Learning to Forgive

Learning to Forgive

A Memoir of Doubt and Faith

WALTER R. SMITH

RESOURCE *Publications* • Eugene, Oregon

LEARNING TO FORGIVE
A Memoir of Doubt and Faith

Copyright © 2009 Walter R. Smith. All rights reserved. Except for brief quotations in critical publications or reviews, no part of this book may be reproduced in any manner without prior written permission from the publisher. Write: Permissions, Wipf and Stock Publishers, 199 W. 8th Ave., Suite 3, Eugene, OR 97401.

Resource Publications
An Imprint of Wipf and Stock Publishers
199 W. 8th Ave., Suite 3
Eugene, OR 97401

www.wipfandstock.com

ISBN 13: 978-1-60608-836-4

Manufactured in the U.S.A.

Scripture references are quoted from:
Revised Standard Version of the Bible, copyright 1952 [2nd edition, 1971] by the Division of Christian Education of the National Council of the Churches of Christ in the United States of America. Used by permission. All rights reserved.
New Revised Standard Version Bible, copyright 1989, Division of Christian Education of the National Council of the Churches of Christ in the United States of America. Used by permission. All rights reserved.

To my family with love
and
In loving memory of Jackie Hatch

Contents

List of Images ix
Acknowledgments xi
Preface: The Sins of the Fathers xiii

1 I Believe, But Why? 1

2 The Promise 15

3 Beauty and the Beast 31

4 The Jesus Nut 42

5 It's Not Easy Being Small 68

6 No Place to Hide: The Call to the Ministry 83

7 Dad, No Dad 115

8 I Give Up, God: Forgiving My Mother 128

Epilogue 147
Appendix: The Struggle of the Soul, A Sermon 149

List of Images

Sally Smith, the author's mother at age 20 / 63
Sally Smith in her late 20s / 63
Sadie Black, the author's grandmother at age 18 / 64
John Black, the author's grandfather / 64
Guy Lombardo, the author, Walter C. Smith, the author's father / 65
Guy Lombardo and Walter C. Smith with trumpet
 and mellophone / 65
Walter C. Smith playing the mellophone with Lombardo's
 Royal Canadians / 66
The only picture I have of my father smiling / 66
Kenny Sargent / 67

Acknowledgments

NO BOOK IS POSSIBLE just as no life is possible without the help of many people along the way. The following people have been God's gift to me:

My wife, Maureen, who encouraged me to continue writing even when I doubted I had anything to say, and who was my first reader and editor. Jackie Hatch. Ross Greek, who was a father to me when I needed it the most, and who showed me what it meant to be a Christian.

Dewey Ajoika, my English professor in college, who encouraged me to keep writing even though I got an "F" on my first assignment. My Algebra teacher, whose name I forget, but whose words I will never forget: "The neatness of your work makes me glad you joined my class." Joe, whose words I hated at the time, but who led me closer to the path God set for me. I hope you became a great doctor. The members of West Hollywood Presbyterian Church, who loved and accepted this young boy and saw more in me than I could see in myself. My Doctor of Ministry Advisor, Gordon Lathrop, who opened my eyes to the deeper meaning of scriptures that gave me the strength to face the dark night of the soul. Beata Cronin, Marvin Gold, Howard Doerle, Ed Stevens, and Ted Stein: my counselors and mainstays of support throughout a long struggle to forgive and find hope in life. They asked me the tough questions I did not want to hear, but to my surprise, they were healing questions. Carolyn Walker, my faithful critic and friend who tells me not what I want to hear, but what I need in order to be a better writer, and who always has an encouraging word. Allan Duane, Ralph Keyes, Musa Meyer, Susan Perry, Gloria Kempton, Christine Lareau, and Kathie Giorgio who were faithful instructors and critics of my writing. Clem Lamberth, my former boss, who died a day before his sixtieth birthday: "You demanded excellence, you untied my hands, and you let me soar. No head pastor ever did that before and none has since. I miss you; the church misses you."

Naomi and Colin Caldwell, dear friends in the ministry, who were early readers of this book, and made invaluable suggestions. Pat Sova, a fellow counselor and friend who read the manuscript with critical love. Charlie Davidson, dear friend and colleague, who painstakingly edited this manuscript and made invaluable suggestions for making it better. Ann Loomis, a dear friend, a fellow journey person on the road of Jungian psychology, and an enthusiastic and creative writer with an eagle's eye for detail who helped in its editing. Jim Tedrick, Managing Editor, Diane Farley, Editorial Administrator, and all the other good folks at Wipf and Stock for their help and competency in publishing this book.

My mother Sally, my father Walter, and grandmother, Sadie: "While you gave me more problems than help, you had the wisdom to have me baptized into the Christian faith, and in so doing you gave me the greatest gift of all—the power of God, in Christ, to live and die in this world, with hope."

AUTHOR'S NOTE

Memoir seeks to tell emotional truth. While the scenes in this book happened, a few did not happen in the order in which they appear. In the scene where my mother, father, and I are in Las Vegas (chapter 4), sitting at a table and receiving guests, the names of the guests are fictitious, because I do not remember them, but the conversations are accurate. Also, the presence of Kenny Sargent is made up. My mother spoke of him so many times and used endearing words to describe him that I had to get him into the story in some way, and this was the best way I could do it. I never met Sargent, and if my memory serves me correctly, my mother told me he died at a young age sometime in the late 1930s or early 1940s. Also, some names have been changed.

Preface

The Sins of the Fathers

"WHO SINNED, THIS MAN or his parents that he was born blind?" the disciples ask Jesus in the ninth chapter of the Gospel of John as they encounter the blind man. Jesus answers that neither the man nor his parents sinned: "He was born blind so that God's works might be revealed in him."[1] I understand what Jesus is saying. Our physical illnesses and disabilities are not the result of our sins or the sins of our parents. God doesn't punish us by making us sick or disabled.

I could argue, though, that in another respect, the parents' sins are passed along to their children. My father, Walter C. Smith, smoked two packs of cigarettes a day. It took me until my mid-forties to stop having serious yearly bouts with asthmatic bronchitis, which was the result of my contact with second-hand smoke. He was raised by brutal parents who, when he was small, whipped him on his bare flesh with a cat-o-nine tails, and hit him on his face and head so hard that his ears bled. While he never lifted a hand to me, he was nevertheless an ineffectual father. He neglected me, we rarely spoke, and I grew up doubting his love and my ability to face the world.

My mother, Sally Smith, conflicted over her relationship with her husband and her own father, made me her "little man" with all the rights and none of the privileges. She put her hand up my pants several times a month, under the guise of adjusting my underwear. Sometimes she did this when we were alone, but most times in view of girls my own age, or in front of other women. I was terrified—afraid she would expose me by pulling my pants down. She created in me a mistrust of women and serious doubts about my ability to relate to them.

1. John 9:1–3.

It took me sixty angry years (I'm sixty-five as I write this) to overcome the sins of my parents. During that time, I lost my faith in God. That's hard for me to admit since I'm a Presbyterian minister. I was able to regain my faith, however. I came to understand that I couldn't get to the resurrection without first going through the crucifixion. I also learned that Jesus was right when Peter asked how many times must we forgive, and he replied, ". . . seventy times seven."[2]

---

2. Matt 18:22

1

I Believe, But Why?

The wolf shall dwell with the lamb, and the leopard shall lie down with the kid, and the calf and the lion and the fatling together, and a little child shall lead them.

Isa 11:6

MY FAITH HAS OFTEN led to more questions than answers, more doubts than certainties, and my relationship with God has been more like living through a hurricane than dwelling in a peaceful, pastoral scene. What I thought faith in God would help me with didn't. I had to rethink my relationship with God and see God in new ways that at first seemed alien and contradictory. Parents are supposed to be a conduit to God for their children; mine were often an impediment, the ones who argued against my having faith. I'm not saying this to get you to hate my parents because I have probably been an impediment to my own children's faith. Children who grow up with a parent, who is a pastor, as mine did, usually witness the negative aspects of serving the church while not seeing many of the positive. When their parent comes under criticism from the church, and it is cruel at times, and is asked to leave the church, children do not understand what is happening and tend to see the church as an institution that is hurting the mother or father they love. Pastors also tend to share their frustrations of church work with their families, and sometimes too much. It is no wonder children of pastors often grow up not liking the church.

While neither of my parents were pastors, their abuse and neglect of me was devastating as was their hostility to my becoming a pastor. Instead of providing me with security in life, they created in me doubts that confirmed my inadequacy—a view of myself that I reasoned was also shared by God. As I struggled with those doubts, I wondered where God was. I sought to serve God to the best of my ability but I often thought God wasn't helping me. It was as if God were saying, "I don't care about you—just do my will." I remember a song in the musical "1776," where John Adams is singing, "Is anybody there, does anybody care, does anyone see what I see?"[1] Just change the words "anybody" and "anyone" to "God" and you have my questions.

In spite of my questions and doubts, I can't remember a time when my relationship with God wasn't important in my life. Even as a child I believed in God, though I am not quite sure why. Why did I believe when others who had similar experiences to mine didn't? Where did my faith come from? How does faith begin and what is it about faith that allows a person to overcome hardships and forgive unforgivable sins?

Are we born with faith or does it develop over the years? Maybe it is a combination of both—much like anything we do well. Athletes have to have certain innate talents to be good athletes, but unless they practice constantly, their talent never develops. Alternatively, maybe faith is a gift that is given to us by people in our past as kind of an inheritance; the product of someone else's labor of which we are the beneficiaries. Might faith and its development be as mysterious and wondrous as the development of our bodies from the moment of conception to the time we return to dust?

My first experience of church that I remember was in a Sunday School room in the basement of the First Presbyterian Church in Glen Cove, Long Island, New York. The building was an old, brown and white Tudor structure set on a grassy hill near Brewster Street, the main street into and out of town. It was raining that day and there were buckets on the floor to catch the water dripping from the ceiling. The mildew seemed to be reinvigorated with life as its pungent odor passed under our nostrils. The windows were set high in the wall since most of the basement was underground. The only thing I could see as I looked outside was the dark gray sky that mirrored the dimly lit room. During my years as a Presbyterian minister, church architects told me that you need bright, cheerful rooms for children so that they will want to come back. If that is the case, and I don't doubt it, then I should have been turned off of the church from that experience, but I wasn't. Looking back, I view my first

---

1. Peter Stone and Sherman Edwards. "Is Anybody There, 1776: A Musical Play." Penguin Plays, New York, NY, 1976.

experience in church as an apt metaphor for my life. For most of my years, I struggled with the darkness of faith; trying to reconcile my belief in a good and loving God and a God who allows suffering, especially mine, to happen.

Perhaps it was my Sunday School teacher who was glad to see me and made me feel welcomed that kept my interest. It could also have been the pastor of the church, Ward Gypson, who tipped his black fedora to my mother when we met him on the street in downtown Glen Cove one fall day in 1948. I thought it was a kindly act, but he surprised me when he stopped and talked with us. He spoke mostly to my mother then he asked, "And, how do you like school, Walter?" I felt valued: this important man wanted to know how this child liked school, and he knew my name.

Maybe I believed because my grandmother was always telling me of my baptism.

"You were baptized in the Church on the Hill in Flushing, New York. It was a Dutch Reformed Church. The minister who baptized you was a devout Christian and he went to the mission field six months after he baptized you."

I discovered recently, through church records, that the minister who baptized me, the Reverend Bradley J. Folensbee, was the first pastor of the church and retired from there. While he did not go into the mission field, he had served as a missionary to Native Americans earlier in his career.

I got the impression that my grandmother thought highly of this minister, and that my baptism was sufficiently important to her to never ceased telling me about it. There must be something to this baptism, I thought. I couldn't remember it, and other than providing my grandmother with a good story to pass on to her grandson, I couldn't see what a few drops of water sprinkled on my head did for me. Maybe she hoped it would help my faith to develop. What impressed me about her telling me about my baptism was her admiration for the minister who baptized me, and that being a minister was important. The way she spoke of his self-sacrifice in going to the mission field and his devotion to his faith reminds me of people who admired my being a minister because it was something they couldn't do themselves—they see in me the commitment to the faith they wish they had, but don't. Could my grandmother's admiration of this man have been the beginning of God's calling me to the ministry? Was God planting a seed that helped me feel good about the ministry so that when God finally did call, God's call would fall on receptive ears?

Maybe I believe because of the place of my baptism. Flushing has a long history of faith expression and religious tolerance. Chartered by the Dutch West India Company in 1645, it was first named Vlissinger, after the city by the same name in the southwestern Netherlands. The Dutch Reformed Church, strict Calvinists, settled the area. Quakers, The Society of Friends, came to Flushing in the 1650s and found wide acceptance among the people despite the opposition of the Dutch Reformed Church and the Governor, Peter Stuyvesant, who established laws to prevent the Quakers from gathering as a religious group. Henry Townsend, a respected citizen of Flushing, held a Quaker meeting in his house and was arrested, fined, and banished from the community. This caused an uprising among the citizens, which led to "The Flushing Remonstrance," a document demanding religious freedom. It's considered to be the precursor of Amendment I (freedom of religion) in the Bill of Rights of the Constitution of the United States of America.[2]

I'm reminded of Moses giving his farewell address to the Israelites in Deuteronomy. He says nothing about individual faith. His entire discourse is about the faith of the community. Moses believed that the faith of the community transcended and nurtured the faith of the individuals in that community. Was I then the recipient of the faith of this community in which I was baptized? Did the lives of those who lived before me create another womb in which I was formed in the image of God? Did I believe because others before me believed and were willing to stand up and demand religious freedom?

On the other hand, maybe my faith is rooted in my biology. Dr. Timothy Johnson in his book, *Finding God in the Questions*, indicates that there is now scientific evidence that the brain may be hard-wired to believe in God, that we are naturally religious and given to faith from the moment we are born.[3] That would tie into my Presbyterian heritage, which talks about predestination. Could it be that I was predestined to believe in God? In the baptism of an infant, we say that God loves this child even before the child knows God. The implication is that God is already at work in the child long before the child will be cognizant of the presence of God.

---

2. Flushing, Queens, Wikipedia, The Free Encyclopedia.

3. Johnson, Dr. Timothy, *Finding God in the Questions: A Personal Journey*, Downers Grove: Intervarsity Press, 2004, 67.

God says to the prophet Jeremiah in the Bible, "Before I formed you in the womb, I knew you, and before you were born I consecrated you..."[4] There were many times Jeremiah wanted to be free of God. His life was endangered numerous times. Because he suffered greatly for his belief, he is often called the Jesus Christ of the Old Testament. But he could never escape from God.

While I cannot begin to compare myself to Jeremiah, I've never been able to escape from the call of God either. Call it what you will, but I've always felt that God had a tractor beam on me. Something invisible was attached to me that would not let me go. No matter how many times I tried to convince myself I didn't need God, I failed. Even during my ministry, I tried to get out of it by thinking of other occupations I could have enter. I could be a physician, but then I remembered I failed chemistry in college. I could be a teacher, but then I would not be able to sit with people while they died and needed the reassurance that God was with them, which I could give. I could be a salesperson selling a valuable product that would help people to live better lives, but then people wouldn't tell me their innermost fears and problems and trust me to share them only with God. I also couldn't help people to deal with the most perplexing problem of all, suffering. While I could not take their suffering away or tell them why they were suffering, I could give them the hope that as God brought Noah, his family, and the animals safely through the Flood, God would also bring them through their floods. I found meaning in being with people in their most vulnerable and painful times, and the fact that I could find no other profession so fulfilling gave me the assurance that I was right where God wanted me to be—in the ministry.

Maybe I believe in God because of my experience with adversity at a young age. My first experience with death that I remember came in 1952, when I was ten years old and in the fifth grade. Jackie Hatch, my best friend, and I were wrestling on the grounds of what was then called the Port Washington Elementary School in Port Washington, New York, during recess on the Monday of the last week in school. The school was set on a corner lot and we were on the front lawn of the school that faced toward downtown on Port Washington Boulevard. In front of us was a baseball field that the Little League used during the summer. Jackie played one of the outfield positions for one of the teams, if my memory serves

---

4. Jer 1:5.

me correctly. The commercial section of downtown started on the next block below the school. On the corner was a barbershop where I got my haircut for ninety cents plus a dime tip to the barber who was a young, thin, black-haired man who talked little during the haircut. Next to it was a drug store with a soda fountain where we would go for ice cream sodas, comic books, and to buy the newest creation in writing instruments—the Paper Mate ballpoint pen. Up to 70,000 words without refilling (as if anyone would count) was the promise from the company along with no more ink stained shirts from leaky fountain pens that I am sure was a godsend to many a mother and wife. As we wrestled, the warm June breeze flowed across our bodies as effortlessly as the other children laughed and played. I could see the green leaves on the trees dance in excitement as the wind caressed their faces. Excitement was everywhere as Jackie and I rolled around on the thick green grass knowing that school would soon be over for the year. He pinned me, sat on my chest with his knees on my arms, and we both laughed. The bright blue sky framed his black hair and slender face. I thought to myself that Jackie was going be a fine man when he grew up. I don't know why I thought that. As I look back on it now, it was a mature thought and one that you would not expect from a ten year old.

Jackie and I were opposites in many ways. He was a good athlete, I was not. He was popular and could move in and out of circles of friends with ease while I, in my shyness, felt uncomfortable around people not always knowing what to say or do and fearing the ridicule that came from other kids about my size or athletic ability. When it came to choosing sides for softball, Jackie would be the first chosen, and I, the last. One day we played on opposite teams and it was my turn to bat.

"Hey, Shrimp is up at bat. You outfielders can all come in and take a nap," one of the players on the opposing team shouted.

The first pitch came in and I swung and missed. I did the same on the next one.

"Ah, come on, throw the kid a ball he can hit," the third basemen said.

The pitcher moved in from the pitcher's mound to where he was only about fourteen feet in front of me. His next ball came in soft, right across the plate. It looked like it almost stopped in mid-air so that I could hit it. I swung as hard as I could. A loud crack reverberated through the air as my bat hit the ball. For an instant, my eyes closed and my world turned eerily silent as I shut out the clamoring noises of the baseball field, my feelings of inferiority, and dwelt on the vision of the ball going over the heads of the outfielders and my rounding the bases in a victory lap. Instead, the ball hit the ground about ten feet in front of me and rolled gently into the pitcher's glove. He picked it up, walked over to first base, and arrived there a few seconds before I did running at full speed. It was the third out. As the kids laughed at me, I picked up my glove and headed toward the outfield. I passed Jackie coming in and was embarrassed I had failed in front of my friend. Yet, as I looked at him, there was no disappointment evident on his face and no word of ridicule ever came from his mouth.

Jackie wasn't in school the next day or the rest of the week. Our teacher told us that he was sick and in the hospital. I didn't think much of it. My mind was more on whether or not I would be promoted to the sixth grade. All that week I prayed myself to sleep, pleading with God to let me be promoted. When I woke up on Friday, I feared the worst—that I would have to repeat the fifth grade. What made me so anxious, I don't know because I had passing grades all through the year. But I also didn't like my teacher and the thought of having to spend another year with her was frightening.

I went to my classroom and it seemed that everything such as taking attendance and saying the pledge of allegiance took longer to do than any other time. We were only going to be in school until noon but the minutes passed so slowly that it felt like a whole day ahead of us. Finally, near the end of the morning our teacher handed out the report cards in alphabetical order. With the name of "Smith," I was almost next to last. I finally got my report card and looked on the back where it said, "The student is hereby promoted to sixth grade." I breathed a sigh of relief. My worst fears hadn't come true—oh thank you, God. Now I was ready for the bell to so that I could begin my carefree summer that kids enjoyed in the early 1950s. The teacher became quiet and asked for our attention. She bowed her head, and said, "Class, I'm afraid I have some bad news for you. Jackie Hatch died last night." Jackie died? She must be kidding. Jackie couldn't have died; we were just wrestling a few days ago and he was in perfect health. No, this is not real.

The bell rang and I ran to my bike and rode home as fast as I could. I burst into the house sobbing and screaming, "Jackie died." At first, my grandmother was bewildered—she didn't understand what I was saying and she didn't know much about Jackie and our friendship. She held my sobbing body until I could tell her that Jackie, my best friend, had died.

Oh, God, why did you let him die? God, I'd be willing to repeat fifth grade if that's what it would take to bring him back. I sobbed all afternoon and the next day. I didn't understand death. What happens when you die? Do you just cease to exist? Will I ever see Jackie again?

The next day it rained. My mother was going to take me to the funeral home to see his body. I was in my room on the second floor in my underwear looking out the window at the gray sky. I didn't want to get dressed; I was afraid of what I would see at the funeral home. Afraid that I could die, too, and no one would remember me. Maybe that's why I remember Jackie to this day. My eyes were drawn to the sunflower in the back yard. On sunny days, it stood tall and erect with its bright face making even a bright day brighter. But today it drooped as raindrops fell from it petals. I thought of my aunt who died six years earlier, and the story that the family liked to tell about me when I saw her body. I said to them, "Shsh, she's sleeping." I didn't remember that incident, but I knew I would never forget my first friend who died. What I didn't know was how I would react on seeing my friend dead. Would I be allowed to touch him? What would he feel like? Would I even want to touch him?

I turned my head away from the window when I heard my grandmother come into my room. She stood beside me and together we looked out the window. I felt her arm around my shoulder as she said, "Happy are the dead that the rain rains on." I didn't know what she meant. How can a dead person be happy? And why does rain produce that happiness? As I look back now, I realize she was trying her best to help me with my grief. I'm sure my constant sobbing was difficult for my family to handle since there was not much they could do. Yet, her saying that gave me some hope. Maybe Jackie was happy. Maybe he wasn't totally gone.

My mother parked the car in the funeral home's parking lot in the rear and we walked to the front of the redbrick building punctuated with large white windows with small, rectangular clear panes of glass. It seemed huge as we walked up several concrete steps to a big white door framed by two white Roman columns. As the door opened, a man in a black suit said, "Good afternoon, may I help you?" My mother told him we were here to see Jackie Hatch. He pointed to the room immediately to our right and I looked in. Right in front of me was his casket. The young boy lying so still in his last bed seemed so far away I thought it would take me an hour to get to him. As I came closer, I couldn't recognize him. Oh good, they made a mistake I thought, it's not Jackie after all, we can go home now. Then I went down to the end of the casket and looked up at him lengthwise and my last hope ended. It was hard for me to imagine that less than a week ago, we were laughing and wrestling with each other, and now he just lay there.

Thoughts of Jackie filled my summer days. I woke every morning wondering where he was or if he was. I wrote his name and date of death, June 19, 1952, in my Bible and stared at it daily. A month after his death, my mother took me to the sporting goods store where they had a trophy, two and a half feet high with a young boy swinging a bat on the top. Mounted on the front of the trophy was a gold plate with the inscription, *The Jackie Hatch Trophy*. I think it was to be given each year to the Little League team that had the best record at the end of the summer. I looked at the trophy for a long time. I imagined Jackie swinging a bat much like the figure on top of the trophy. With my fingers, I traced his name on the gold plate. There was a baseball game played in his honor. I didn't go. I don't why. When I think about it, no one told me when the game was. Someone said that Jackie's team won. When school started that fall, I had my first male teacher, Alvin Leirheimer, who taught us how to square dance, and made us practice our handwriting skills. I also had my first girlfriend, Diane Chrisco, who was my square dance partner. But Jackie wasn't there, and I missed him.

About fifteen years ago, I realized that one of the things that bothered me about Jackie's death was that I didn't know why he had died. A rumor circulated at school that he had died from blood poisoning. I also didn't know where he was buried. I contacted the Port Washington News and found out that he was taken to New Hampshire, his family's home state, for burial. Through the Historical Society in New Hampshire, I was able to contact his brother whose name I forget. He told me that Jackie died of peritonitis. He had had his appendix taken out the year before and the peritonitis had infected the area of the surgery, which was common then. Today we don't hear much about it because we have antibiotics. He also told me that Jackie was buried in an unmarked grave.

I'm astonished that after fifty-five years I still have a vivid memory of Jackie. The view that always comes to mind when I think of him, especially in June, is his laughing face as he sat on top of me. Maybe it's my way of not letting him go; of always wanting him around. It could also be that I have never resolved his death. It came at a time when I was just waking up to the world and to the knowledge that bad things can and do happen, and maybe that's where it will stay. At the time it happened, Jackie's death neither increased nor diminished my belief in God. I wasn't angry with God for taking my friend; I was sad and felt alone. It's only as time has passed that I began to realize the importance of Jackie in my life. Ridicule from other boys was a staple in my diet, but Jackie never ridiculed me. I felt safe with him, and in that safety, I found hope that I was a worthwhile person and that not all would treat me like the others. Jackie's gift to me will last an eternity because Jackie was God's gift to me, and maybe that's why I believe in God.

～

In eighth grade, 1955, I attended Roslyn High School since my parents had moved from Port Washington to Roslyn the year before, a distance of three miles. The first day of school brought temperatures of 75 degrees with clear blue skies. As I walked into the art room, one of the classes I had to take that year, I noticed the sun was sending its sharp rays through the wall of windows on the south side. The room was long and narrow with three rows of drafting desks, two in each row placed side-by-side. We sat on stools to give us enough height to work comfortably on the desks. The teacher's desk was in the front of the room and behind it were three 4'x8' slate blackboards free of any evidence that they had been touched by chalk.

I went into the classroom and sat next to a pretty girl. She had long, black hair, was thin, and had the beginnings of breast development. I wanted to introduce myself to her, but I didn't. The class was a mixture of thirty boys and girls. Some of the boys were complaining that they had to take this stupid class. "Art is for sissies and girls," they said. One of the girls told them to grow up. With the ringing of the bell, our teacher walked into the room. She was petite, had blond hair, blue eyes, and was attractive. I forget her name, so for the purpose of this story I will call her Mrs. Havel. She spoke with a heavy accent that turned her "w's" into "v's" and added "d's" to the end of words that ended in "t."

"Class, I want to introduce myself to you. My name is Mrs. Havel, and I will be your art teacher for the year."

"What did you say?" one of the boys shouted out, imitating her accent. The class erupted in laughter.

"My name is Mrs. Havel, and I will be your art teacher this year."

"I couldn't understand you," the same boy said, drawing more snickers.

"I'm very sorry, class. I come from Hungary, and English is difficult for me."

Over the next several weeks, Mrs. Havel told us how she and several of her girlfriends crawled on their bellies for three weeks to escape from the Communists in 1946. Her father was in the underground resistance to the Soviet Union and had disappeared just before she and her girlfriends decided to escape. She had been in America for eight years and she had not heard anything from her family even though she wrote them constantly. The boys in the class continued to ridicule her manner of speech and they refused to do anything she asked. One day she came into class and on the blackboard, the boys had written, *Communist*. She left the room in tears as she had on other days. I refused to ridicule her. After she left the room, the boys turned on me.

"Well, what the hell is wrong with you, sissy Walter? You don't like her anymore than we do, yet you don't say a word. Don't you like us?"

"I like her, I think she's a good teacher," I said.

"Oh, the sissy's in love with her. I bet he wants to feel her boobs and between her legs, and screw her."

"Naw," said another boy. "He hasn't thought of that, because I bet he doesn't know what's between a woman's legs, let alone how to screw her. Do you, sissy?" I said nothing.

"Well, tell us and tell the girls what's between their legs."

I felt I had been stripped naked. I had never been in a situation where sex was the subject and girls were present and listening. It was embarrassing to hear talk about boobs, what was between a woman's legs, and screwing. But what was more embarrassing was that by my silence I had admitted to the whole class that outside of boobs, I knew nothing more about a woman's body.

After the Thanksgiving holiday, five of the boys surrounded my desk again. They had been bragging in class that their parents were trying to get Mrs. Havel fired because she wasn't a good teacher.

"Either you go along with us and help us to get this bitch of a teacher fired or we'll beat the shit out of you," they said.

I was frightened. They were stronger and outnumbered me, and from our encounter about sex, had intimidated me. Every day from then on, I ran to the school bus to get on it as quickly as I could, even pushing myself ahead of the girls.

"Can you imagine that," I heard one of the girls say. "Look at that, he has no manners." But I didn't care. I was safe and would be home soon.

The kids I feared the most in school, the kids who threatened me, were the good kids. They went to church or synagogue and their fathers were deacons, elders, and council members of their local congregations. The kids I should have feared, but didn't, were the black kids and the white hoodlums, the ones who wore black motorcycle jackets and carried six inch blade knives in their black boots. To them I was a friend. One night, I went to the movies with my mother and grandmother. In the lobby, several of my friends were there.

"Hey, Whitey how ya doin? It's good to see you."

"I'm fine."

"Is this your mother?"

"Mom, Nana, I want you to meet my friends. This is Joey, Tony, and Damani."

"Good to meet you Mrs. Smith and Mrs. Black. You've got a nice son."

They started to go into the theater as did I, but my mother grabbed me by the arm and pulled me back.

"Do you run around with trash like that at school? You need to be careful of yourself."

"I've never been so scared in all my life," my grandmother said.

"They're good kids, Mom. They don't give me any trouble."

At the end of the eighth grade, I was walking in the courtyard of the school. It was a warm sunny day and I was happy that it was the last day of school. I heard my art teacher calling my name.

"Walter, Walter," she said in her heavy accent, running up to me. "I want you to know I'm leaving teaching. You don't know how much you have meant to me this year."

"I'm sorry, you're a good teacher."

"Thank you, but I can't take the ridicule anymore. You were the only boy who didn't make fun of me. You gave me hope to get through the year. I can't tell you how much you mean to me. I will never forget you."

Her words overwhelmed me. I came to school everyday cowered by the hostility of some of my fellow students, and I made myself as inconspicuous as possible. I felt powerless and worthless. I felt that if I was any sort of a "guy" I would have told those boys to go to hell and learned karate so I could defend myself. But I didn't. I shrunk in the face of fear.

Now my teacher was telling me I was more powerful than I thought, but it was a different kind of power; it was a power that could bring hope to another person.

As I look back on it now, I can see that the suffering we both experienced was something that didn't have to be the final word in life; that there was a greater power at work and that suffering was the means to unleash such power. I'm reminded of the death and resurrection of Jesus Christ. Jesus was crucified publicly and all were able to see him in agony on the cross. However, the resurrection was for *members only*. Jesus appeared to only a few of his followers. My teacher and I were publicly threatened and ridiculed that year, but in those few moments in the courtyard we were alone—no one knew of the victory we had just experienced.

Maybe I believe because I have been able to be with people in their own adversity. In 1967, I was the Assistant Pastor of the Croftfoot Parish Church in Croftfoot, a suburb of Glasgow, Scotland. One of our parishioners, Stewart Brown, had circulation problems. He was in the hospital for surgery, and his surgeon told him he would have to amputate at least half his foot. Stewart was depressed and I thought he was suicidal. I was happy he was in the hospital where he could do no harm to himself. Sometimes, people in hospitals think their situation is worse than it is and I decided to go to see his surgeon. As I was leaving the hospital, I stopped by the operating rooms and asked the nurse if I could talk to Stewart's surgeon. He told me that Stewart's condition was as serious as Stewart said, and he knew he would have to amputate most of his foot. I thanked him for his time and left. The day after surgery, I went back to see Stewart. He was all smiles.

"Well, you seem cheerful today," I said.

"My doctor didn't amputate my foot. When he opened me up there was all nice pink flesh and the circulation was perfect. I thanked my doctor and he said, 'Don't thank me, thank that young minister of yours. No minister has ever come to me concerned about one of my patients. Lately, I've had surgeries that have not turned out well and I felt a failure as a surgeon. But his coming to see me reminded me that I was not the only one in the operating room—that God was with me.'"

Three people came to deeper faith that day. Stewart was reassured that God was with him, as was the surgeon, and I was amazed that God could do so much with so little effort on my part. I spent only about five minutes, if that, with the surgeon, and I never said anything about praying for him nor did I mention God. All through seminary, I'd had visions of doing great things for God and making great sacrifices. I learned that day, that God was the one who did the great things. I only had to open the door and give God the opportunity to work.

Why did God intervene that day? Was it because we were all at a dead-end? We didn't know what more we could do or say. I didn't know what to say to Stewart in his darkest hour. I was a neophyte pastor, and from my past experience I wasn't too sure about what God could or would do. Stewart was without hope, and the surgeon was facing death on a daily basis and could see no way out. Was that why God intervened? Or was it because we were three people questioning if God was really there, if God really cared, and we needed something to quell our doubts? If so, then why doesn't God do the same for others in similar situations?

I also have to question if God really intervened that day or if it was a stroke of good luck. The trouble with miracles is how do we know when they happen? I once had an abscessed tooth. My dentist did a root canal, but the tooth didn't heal. He sent me to an oral surgeon who wanted to take some bone from my upper palate and put it in the infected area to help the healing. I didn't like the idea. He put me on antibiotics and pain medication. A week later when we were to make the final decision, he took another x-ray and found the tooth completely healed. Was that a miracle? Neither of us could understand why this happened, and neither saw it as a miracle. With Stewart's situation, it was different. We were all searching for God in one way or another, and when Stewart's foot was healed, all three of us recognized it as a miracle, and we did so independently, without one of us forcing that conclusion onto the others.

My faith is probably a product of all these experiences. You might have the feeling that my life should be easy from having had all these wonderful faith experiences by the time I was twenty-eight years old. However, remember that I am writing about these experiences many years after they happened, and at a point when I have had time to reflect on their meaning. The truth is that as my life unfolded, the doubts, fears, and pain of the past became formidable adversaries that showed me the futility of faith and led me to condemn God to hell.

2

The Promise

I trace the rainbow through the rain, and feel the promise is not vain, that morn shall tearless be.

"O Love That Wilt Not Let Me Go,"
George Matheson, 1882

The day my father died, I grieved. But I didn't grieve for the loss of a relationship where Dad took me hunting and fishing and we bonded as men who would change the world. Rather, mine was a grief for a relationship that could have been but never was; a grief for a relationship where I had to give up my childhood in order to be my father's father.

The last time I saw my father was six months before his death from Emphysema and Alzheimer's, in May 1992 when I was fifty years old. I didn't know what to expect when I drove up to his apartment in Escondido, California, since we hadn't seen each other in about six years, due to my financial situation and his inability to travel. As I made a left turn onto the six-lane Escondido Boulevard, the sun shown directly into my windshield causing everything in my sight to look as if it was a silhouette. My sunglasses and the sun visor of my car did little to reduce the effect of the sun's rays. About a half a mile ahead of me, I saw a person wandering into the middle of the street as cars streamed by at fifty plus miles an hour and swerved to miss him. No one in his or her right mind would dare to cross this street, I thought. But then I remembered, my father wasn't in his right mind. My God, he's going to be killed before I get to see him, I shouted in the emptiness of my car. I pulled into the driveway of his apartment complex and ran to the street. He had gotten back safely. When he saw me, he threw his arms around me as a drowning man throws his arms around a life preserver. Such display of affection was not a part of my father's repertoire. He had not shaved, and his protruding whiskers rubbed across my face like a wired brush and reminded me of the time, as a child, he tickled me with them and I giggled. He had not smoked for twenty years but his body still had the stale, charred aroma of smoke. His teeth had permanently yellowed, and I could hear him struggling for each breath as he held me tightly. When he pulled back from the embrace, I saw that his once clear eyes were now cloudy. He kept looking at me as if he were trying to bring me into focus. His loss of hair seemed to have stopped, and he had the remnants of the pompadour he had always combed straight back, only now the dark brown hair had turned gold. He walked slowly and with a shuffle.

"I'm no good anymore, Walter. I can't do a thing for myself," he said as we walked between the cacti that bordered the walk to his apartment. I put my arm around him and held him tight, trying to hold back the tears that had welled up in my eyes. His statement was piercing. As a minister, I had heard the same statement from other older people. It comes from a belief that a person's validity and worth are dependent upon their being able to produce and take care of themselves—a false, but understandable, belief in my view. I'm always shocked when older people tell me this, but now those words were coming from my own father. How can you say that, Dad, I thought, when I need you so much? Don't you care about me? You still have lots to do—I still need a father.

He and his wife, my stepmother (my parents were divorced when I was twenty), took me to lunch at Lawrence Welk's resort. As we entered through the heavy wooden doors of the restaurant, I immediately felt the difference in the air conditioning. In the desert, to cool the air, water vapor is added through swamp coolers as opposed to humid climates where water is taken out of the air. The air is cool but moist. We were given a table by the window where I could see the light brown rolling hills dotted with cacti. It was a barren land with a piece of life here and a piece of life there with no visible connection. It reminded me of my life with my father, and I wondered if that was the way my father experienced his life. Unexpectedly, he began to talk.

"That tape you sent me really meant a lot. It was a very mature thing to do," he said.

I had sent him a tape nine months earlier in which I shared with him the good things about our lives and how proud I was that he was my father. It wasn't totally a mature thing to do. I did it more for myself than for him. He had called me one Sunday to tell me he had been diagnosed with Alzheimer's. While he was not in the advanced stages, he was not in the early stages either. I knew I didn't have long before he wouldn't be able to understand what I was saying.

All my life, I had wanted him to tell me how proud he was of me. My father was an enigmatic figure, a man of few words who never shared what he was thinking. Smiles never came quickly or easily for him. I knew when he was smiling because I could see part of his upper teeth and his mouth looked a little broader. Other than that, his face always looked the same. This created confusion in me as to where I stood in his life. Was he proud of me? As a child with a child's mind, I automatically assumed that if he didn't tell me he was, it meant he wasn't.

Because children take responsibility for everything that happens to them, I knew it was my fault that my father was not proud of me. It didn't take much for me to think that if I was such a disappointment to my earthly father, how much more of a disappointment was I to my heavenly father?

My pastor, who was more of a father to me than my own father was, told me he was proud of me, and I basked in that glory, but it wasn't enough. Now, I was panic-stricken. What would happen if my father died and I never got to hear those words I so desperately needed to hear? Could I continue to live? If I didn't receive my father's blessing, would I ever be able to get God's? If I couldn't influence my father, which should be infinitely easier, how could I ever expect to influence God? If God didn't affirm me, what hope would I have? So, I sent the tape hoping that as I told him how proud I was of him, he would take the hint and tell me how proud he was of me, but he never did.

After his death, I wrote a short story about his lack of approval of me, which was published in the Christian Science Monitor under the title, *A Son Seeks A Father's Approval*.[1]

The title was not my choice but the editor's. I didn't think about it at the time, but the word "Father's" could be interpreted in two ways—earthly or heavenly father. The editor got it right—I was seeking both Fathers' approval.

My stepmother showed the article to some of their friends. A woman wrote me and berated me for thinking my father was not proud of me.

---

1. *Christian Science Monitor,* "A Son Seeks A Father's Approval", September 27, 1995, 16.

"You are the only one of his family he ever talked about," she said. "He was so proud that you were a minister."

I thought, after all these years, his words of approval had to come from a total stranger. I wondered why he couldn't tell me the things he told others about me. As I look back now, I begin to think of the times I've told my sons that I'm proud of them. Tears stream from my eyes; words choke up in my throat. I'm vulnerable. I can't speak clearly so I just put my arms around them and let my tears run down my cheeks. I'm laying my soul on the line, hoping they will accept my love. It makes it harder for me when I realize that my sons are not men who go in for such sentimental displays of affection. I've had to learn other ways to tell them I'm proud of them, to reveal what I feel in my heart so that they can hear what I'm saying with their minds. Maybe I didn't think my father was proud of me because my father never learned to put the words that were in his mind into words that would resonate with my heart.

"Everyone needs a boost in life and that really gave me a boost. I've listened to it over and over again," he said. Okay, Dad. Now give me a boost, I thought. I did for you what you should've done for me a long time ago. I'm teaching you how to be a father, Dad.

After lunch, I went into the card store to buy some postcards to send to my wife and sons. When I came out my father seemed upset. His eyes were fixed and looked straight into the store.

"What's the matter, Dad?" I said.

"It's disgusting," he said. "Look at all those people having sex in there."

I looked back into the card shop to see what I had missed. Then, I realized I was seeing a part of his Alzheimer's. I was scared that the rest of the day might be like this and we wouldn't have the opportunity to be father and son. I still had a few more hours to get him to say he was proud of me, but now that was in jeopardy. First Presbyterian Church of Lynchburg, Virginia, was sending me on a goodwill visit to another church in Taiwan and I had to leave the next day. I knew there was a good chance I would never see him again. I didn't have the money to fly back to California from my home in Virginia. My wife and I had high medical bills that insurance didn't cover, two children to care for, and neither of us was making a lot of money. In fact, the only way I was seeing him now was that the church was paying my way to Taiwan and I could stop over in Los Angeles for an additional seventy-five dollars. On the other hand, I was amused he could mention sex. He had been embarrassed when he had to explain to me when I was fifteen the purpose of a condom, and he never did mention masturbation.

We returned to his apartment and my stepmother went swimming, leaving my father and me alone on the balcony to enjoy the warm sun and each other's presence.

My father had been a professional musician with many of the big bands in the Big Band Era: Guy Lombardo, Larry Clinton, Glenn Gray and the Casaloma Orchestra, and Isham Jones. I wanted to know some things about him that others had told me but he never had. On a few occasions, people outside of our family had told me how great a musician he was and how he was respected for his high moral standards. My father not only didn't tell me what he thought, he never spoke of his work or his childhood. And like sex, we never talked about right and wrong. Our relationship reminded me of the times I went fishing. When I hooked a fish, there was first the excitement of feeling the pull on the string, and then there was the anticipation of seeing what I caught. It could be a sand shark, a stingray, or a good-sized black sea bass or flounder. With my father, I had the excitement of the pull on the string—I did have a father. But I never got him to the surface. I didn't know whether or not to celebrate my catch or throw it back in. I felt alone in the world. There was a world out there, but without knowing who my father was, I felt I had no connection to it. So I had to know who he was. I had to know if there was anyone at home in his body, not so much for his sake, but for mine. I had to know if my origins were real or imaginary.

"Dad, didn't you play with the NBC Symphony Orchestra in the late 1930s?" I asked.

"Yeah, I played with the radio orchestra, not the one under Toscanini, but the one that did the radio shows."

"That must have been quite an experience," I said.

"I remember one time when there was a trumpet solo. There were three trumpeters in the orchestra. When the other two saw how difficult the piece was they walked off the stage. It was left for me to play it."

"What happened?"

"Oh, I played the solo." Then he choked and tears started flowing from his eyes. "When I got through, all the string players stood up and tapped their bows on their music stands. That was the highest compliment they could give another musician, especially a brass man."

I was stunned—I had never seen my father cry. Then my feelings turned to joy. He was real, he was a good musician, his music did make a difference in his life, and he was proud of it. Tears streamed down my face, too. I reached over and we embraced, paving the way for our tears to flow together.

"You've a lot to be proud of, Dad," I said. We were silent for a while, basking in the glory of a moment that affirmed for my father his contribution to life. As we talked and reminisced, we laughed and cried, and it seemed that I was meeting my father for the first time. I grieved. On one hand, I was overjoyed that I was a part of this man who was an accomplished musician. On the other hand, I was angry. Damn it, Dad, I thought. Why have you waited so long to reveal yourself to me? Do you realize that I've lived fifty years listening to my mother's and my grandmother's negative comments about you? You never gave me anything to help me counteract their diatribes. I grew up thinking I came from rubbish, but now I see, even if it is just a glimpse, that I came from gold. Why, God do the good things have to take so long in coming?

The father I knew growing up was silent. When I came home from school, he was usually lying on the couch drinking his third can of beer. I don't think he was an alcoholic even though by five, he had consumed another three cans before driving thirty miles to work at the Roosevelt Hotel in New York City as the second trumpeter of the Guy Lombardo Orchestra. We said, "Hi," to each other, and then I went to my room and didn't see him until we met for our "silent" dinners my grandmother prepared. At 5:30 pm he left with a simple "goodbye" for his nighttime rendezvous with those wishing to dance the hours away.

One day, when I was about twelve, he took me to New York City. Lombardo wanted the band to have new tuxedos and he was footing the bill. I was so excited that I was going to spend a whole day with my father that I could hardly sleep the night before. I watched in awe as the tailor draped the tuxedo cloth over my father, standing in his T-shirt and boxer shorts. He measured my father's shoulders, chest, arms, waist, and legs, making marks on the cloth with white chalk and holding it together with what seemed like a million pins. After the fitting, Dad took me to several music stores to pick up his trumpet that had been repaired and other music paraphernalia. We were greeted warmly in every store. Everyone knew him and his picture was on the walls of these stores. When people found out I was taking piano lessons they said, "If you're half as good of a pianist as your father is a trumpeter, you'll be a fine musician." Half as good, I thought. You mean my father is that good? I felt proud that others respected my father. He wasn't the loser my mother had told me he was.

Dad then took me to the Empire State Building for lunch. I ordered a cream cheese and jelly sandwich, and when it came I noticed the cream cheese had been sliced in the form of a wedge so that at one end of the sandwich the cream cheese was a third of an inch thick and at the other only about a tenth of an inch. I didn't know how I was going to swallow that much cream cheese. I liked cream cheese, but not in that quantity. I must have appeared shocked. My father looked at me and I looked at him. We both started to laugh.

"Do you want me to cut some of that cream cheese off for you?"

"I think you better," I said.

After lunch, we went to the top of the Empire State Building. At that time, it was the tallest building in the world. From the observation deck, I marveled as I looked down and saw cars that I knew were bigger, but from that height, they looked like moving dots on the pavement. We could only see two miles that day because of the haze. But I didn't care. I was on the top of the world with my dad. I had seen a part of my father I'd never seen before. The events of the morning showed me my father was an important person—maybe it meant that I was important too. I was standing next to a great musician, a man who was respected and liked by others, but most importantly a man who was my dad. As I look back on it now, I realize that these impressions of him came largely from others. Our trip home was made in silence, and other than laughing occasionally at the cream cheese and jelly sandwich, we never talked about our trip to New York.

In June, 2003, my wife, Maureen, and I were walking along West 48th Street between 6th and 7th Avenues in New York City when I spotted Manny's Music Store. I immediately recognized it as one of the stores my father had taken me to. "Look, there's Manny's, Maureen. That's one of the stores my father took me took to when I was a kid." I ran across the street almost forgetting to bring Maureen with me. We entered the store. To our left were two young men with black hair helping a customer learn the latest technology of the electric guitar that he was purchasing. There were pictures of musicians on the walls, some obviously old. We looked and looked and there in the back of the store was a picture of my father with some other musicians. He was still a part of New York, I was a part of New York, but more importantly, I was a part of my father. For the first time in my life, I felt I belonged to this world.

Living in the South, with its emphasis on family heritage, is difficult especially when you don't have a family you can point to. Now I did, and that family was surviving the test of time. The clerks in the store were all young men with their computerized and electrified instruments. They probably had never heard of Guy Lombardo. But in the midst of all this generational change my father was there. It was one more thing I could hold on to, one more thing that brought me closer to him and made me glad that, in spite of all our difficulties, he was my father.

~

When my father died, I asked my stepmother if she wanted me to conduct his funeral since I was a minister, and we didn't know a Presbyterian minister in Pennsylvania where he was to be buried. I wanted to do his funeral because I wanted to make sure to the best of my ability that he got into heaven. I wanted to be his advocate before God, and then, maybe, he would realize what a great son he had and regret that he hadn't told me how proud he was of me. But I was, also, hesitant. Ministers are like doctors—we're best when we don't treat our own family. I was in counseling at the time with the Baptist Chaplain of our local hospital, Marvin Gold. He argued against my doing the funeral. "You need the comforting at this time," he said. "You don't need to be the one doing the comforting. This man neglected you. You may have forgiven him, but how can you enter the role of a pastor without doing yourself more harm?"

Gold had a good point, but since my father was to be cremated and buried in Bethlehem, Pennsylvania, and his funeral would not be for another month, I thought I would have time to prepare myself emotionally and spiritually. But, the month proved worrisome. I knew what my mother would think if she found out that I had conducted his funeral, and later I discovered she knew.

All through my life my mother didn't think I should have anything to do with my father. "He never did anything for you," she constantly told me. She was right, but she was also blind to her own form of terrorism, which she unleashed on me at will, and I hated her for reminding me of my absentee father.

My father was also like a dry sponge that soaked up every ounce of water that came within its grasp and gave nothing in return. I had to take the initiative in our relationship. I was the first to say, "I love you." It took him years to say the same words back to me. When he called to tell me of his Alzheimer's, I told him I would like to see him, but we were having financial difficulties and I could only afford about two hundred dollars toward a trip to California where he was living. "Could he help me with the rest?" I said. He called back in a few days saying, "Betty," my stepmother, "and I would love to see you, but we think that it's your responsibility to pay for the ticket." I knew he had the money—they had an affluent lifestyle, and the year before he had paid for my cousin, my stepmother's son, to fly to see them and gave him a thousand dollars. Here was one more thing I had to give, one more thing that was my responsibility. What tore at my heart was that my father didn't think it was important enough to send the money to see me. Apparently, he was willing to die without seeing his son. I felt orphaned before my time.

When I was ordained, he didn't know what to say or how to act around me. "What do I call you, now?" he asked in all seriousness. I had the impression he thought that since I was a "holy man" he should call me "Father, Your Holiness," or "Reverend." I suggested he continue to call me "Walter," since my ordination changed nothing about our being father and son.

When I sent him a gift, he wouldn't mention it until I called and asked him if he got it. There was one time, however, when he called me first. I had sent him an expensive canned ham. It turned out to be rotten.

"What are you doing sending me a rotten ham? Are you trying to tell me something?"

"I didn't know it was rotten, Dad. I'm awfully sorry. I'll send you another one."

"Don't bother," he said, and he hung up.

In 1976, he and Betty visited us in our home in Alexis, Illinois. As we walked up the long sidewalk to the front door, I put my arm around his shoulder.

"Dad, do you remember that day you took me to New York when Lombardo wanted the band to have new tuxes? I was so proud to be your son. People knew you, and it was obvious they thought you were a great musician. I was proud you were my father."

"I was a big man in those days, Walter," he said.

"You're still are a big man in my eyes, Dad."

I thought I saw a tear form in the corner of one of his eyes. If there were other tears, they never materialized and we entered the house in silence. It was an awkward entrance. I had just given my father a high compliment and it felt like it didn't make any difference. Instead, I sensed that my reminding him of that day in New York was as if I were reminding him that he was no longer the man he once was. It didn't make any difference that I saw him in another light. My views weren't important. I felt empty, lost, and impotent.

So, I wondered if, by doing his funeral, I was going too far to get his blessing. Was it becoming an irrational obsession with me? I wondered why I couldn't let it go.

I had other doubts about doing his funeral. Was he saved? I had met many agnostics in my life who seriously doubted the existence of God, but my father allowed no place for God. In my mind, he was a confirmed atheist. Beatings from his parents that left his ears and nose bleeding killed the child before the man was born, and also killed any belief in a loving God. He never received nurturing from his father, so he didn't know how to nurture me. The sins of the fathers are passed on to the sons.

I reread the apostle Paul. In I Corinthians, he advises against divorcing an unbelieving spouse because the believing spouse can save the unbeliever through his or her holiness.[2] Holiness was contagious, in Paul's opinion. Even before his death, but especially in that month after he died, I prayed hard. "God, my father doesn't believe, but I believe. Bring him safely home into your ever loving care, and the joy of your presence for my sake and the sake of your son, Jesus Christ."

What am I doing? I thought. I'm a Presbyterian minister. I don't believe in a vengeful God. Yes, John Calvin, the Father of Presbyterianism, said we are all predestined and that some are predestined to be saved and others are not. But he was also a lawyer who couldn't escape his own logic. If some are saved then it's only logical that some are not. For most of his life, Calvin talked about the love, forgiveness, and redemption of God, not about who was saved and who was not saved. He was also trying to get the people of his day to forget about their salvation and get busy helping those who were powerless and had no hope.

My heart overruled my head, however, and I worried about my father's salvation. As I was revising this section of this book, I began to

---

2. 1 Cor 7.

wonder who I was worried for: was it for my father or was it for me? If God didn't save him, wasn't that between God and him? It wouldn't have any effect on my salvation for God wouldn't hold me responsible for what my father did or didn't do. And I'm sure that God could make it so that I could have eternal life without my father. But there was the rub. At the time of my father's death, I needed and wanted my father. I knew enough about him in spite of his neglect of me to see his goodness and love, and I wanted to have the opportunity to remain father and son and to have it for all eternity. I was angry with my father that he didn't give me that joy on earth. And even though I couldn't express it at the time, I now realize I was more angry with God—the great almighty, omnipotent, all loving God didn't care enough about me to give me what I needed the most. If God didn't save my father, it would mean that God didn't love me. If God really loved me, why did God make it so damn hard to get a little love, a little acceptance? Why did he give me the parents he did? Oh God, our help in ages past, where in the hell are you now?

For many years in our marriage, my wife and I played with each other and sometimes our children a disastrous little game called, *If You Loved Me*. It's disastrous because it always ends in suffering. It goes like this: if you loved me you would make the bed, clean the house, have dinner on time, take the garbage out, give me flowers on my birthday, stop complaining about my not making the bed, never forget our anniversary, get your homework done, keep your room clean, or do what I say. When either of us didn't live up to the other's expectations we were certain the other didn't love us. That led to disagreements and fights and we suffered untold emotional pain. It never crossed our minds that being loved had nothing to do with the other's fulfilling all of our expectations. Likewise, it never crossed my mind that God might love me even though God didn't or couldn't fulfill my expectations. I never thought that maybe God wanted me to have the love of my father and wanted my father to have the love he needed from his parents, but not everyone works for the same thing God wants. We all work out our inner conflicts through our decisions and actions, making it impossible to get what we want or better yet, what God wants. An imperfect lot, we are. Now, I can see that my anxiety over my father's salvation was nothing more than my anxiety over whether or not God loved me. I was sure God didn't, and so I tempted him to prove it. Of course, I would never know the answer to that question until I died, which at the time of my father's death, when I was fifty, meant I probably had a long time to wait and doubt—a long time to suffer. But I wasn't thinking logically—I was angry.

What confused me the most during this time was that I had every reason not to believe in God, but I did. Even on the Sundays I preached, I proclaimed God's love in sermons that on the surface were meant to instill faith in others, but in reality were instilling faith in me—I was preaching to myself. Maybe I knew in the depths of my soul that I was playing this disastrous game with God—tempting God to prove his love for me all the while knowing it would never happen, and I would never be satisfied. Maybe I knew, in the depths of my soul, I was wrong to equate love with another's fulfilling my expectations. Maybe, but on the other hand, I couldn't escape the power of the Gospel story—a story that gave me hope at a time when I didn't think there was any to have. The story wasn't just about God raising a man who lived two thousand years ago from the dead—the story was beginning to become my story. I saw the sufferings of Jesus as my own. When Jesus was ridiculed and scorned, I knew what that was like. Jesus was defenseless against the bullies of the world, and so was I. When Jesus was stripped naked, the flesh ripped off his back with whips, and nailed to the cross, I felt that pain even though I had not experienced his particular form of suffering. And when Jesus cried out on the cross, "My God, my God, why have you forsaken me?"[3] I was screaming those same words, too. And that is where I stayed even though on Sunday the tomb was empty and joy came to Jesus' followers who believed he was risen from the dead—for them defeat had turned into victory and despair into hope. I could feel none of it; I was still on the cross. But the story gave me hope, even though I was angry, that one day I would experience the resurrection. I thought that if I was confused now, God would one day remove that confusion and allow me to see clearly. "For now we see in a mirror dimly, but then face to face. Now I know in part; then I shall understand fully, even as I have been fully understood."[4]

In addition to the sufferings of Jesus, I also remembered that Jesus was the friend of those whom society despised. Tax collectors, prostitutes, lepers, and outcasts were the ones he embraced. He never met a person whom he felt was beyond the redemption and the love of God. When I thought of my father, I saw a man who was disliked by my mother and

---

3. Matt 27:46.
4. 1 Cor 13:12.

her family, and he was poorly received in his own family. My heart went out to him. I saw a lost man who needed to be redeemed, who needed to know that God loved him so much that Jesus died for him, too. I began to find power in my faith and started seeing myself as God's instrument to bring God's redemption to my father. I knew that the only way my father would know about my God and his saving grace in Jesus Christ would be if I showed him even if it meant giving up my life or my mental health to do his funeral. I would have to live out the Gospel story.

I realized that as much as my father needed redemption, I needed it, too. I needed to know if God's love and redemption were real. If I could show my father the love of God by loving him unconditionally and by standing with him even in death, maybe I could show myself God's unconditional love for me. If I could prove it to my father, I could prove it to myself, but the only way for me to prove it was to love even in the midst of my doubts. But my father was dead, so how could I prove such love to him? I couldn't, but I discovered I didn't need to. What became more important was to know that I could be like Jesus and stand with the outcast and the unloved. I could live out the Gospel story, stand with my father in the experience of death as the final outcast, and come to experience the resurrection.

When God was trying to convince Moses to go back to Egypt and bring the children of Israel out of slavery, Moses asked, "Who am I to go to Pharaoh, and bring the Israelites out of Egypt?" God replied, "I will be with you and this shall be the sign for you that it is I who sent you: when you have brought the people out of Egypt, you shall worship God on this mountain."[5] When you think about it, it's no sign at all. Moses had to do the work and then he would know that God was with him. But, in reality, God was always with him. Like Moses, I had to do the work and love my father so I would know that God loved me, but then, I realized, God had always loved me.

Regardless of my faith, it still took every ounce of my being to conduct my father's funeral. As I gave my all, I knew that this time there was no hope of receiving his earthly affirmation. At the end of the funeral, I felt nothing. Relatives remarked how strong I was, "Why he didn't even shed a tear," one of them said. I wasn't strong. I didn't have the strength to cry. I had done all I could do to gain my father's blessing, and to show him he was loved by God. I had done all I could to show God that I could live

---

5. Exo 3:11–12.

out the Gospel story. Now, I knew that I would have to find new meaning to my relationship with my father and God somewhere else or my friend, Marvin, would be right.

~

It was a cool, sunny spring day, late in May, when I arrived at the cemetery to put my father to rest. His grave was about three hundred feet from his parents'. It was on a gently sloping hill framed by a circular driveway. The cemetery superintendent drove up and without saying a word, handed me a box that was wrapped in white paper with raised felt flower designs. It looked like a wedding present but without a bow. At first, I thought it was a gift, but then I realized it was my father's ashes. He was never a big man, but the box made him seem miniscule. So I get to hold you one more time, Dad, I thought. I bent down and gently put the box in the white, polyethylene container surrounded by the black dirt and green grass that was to be his grave. I paused and felt the cool, spring breeze blow against my black clerical robe and white stole, and then I remembered why I was doing his funeral.

I was nine years old and my mother, grandmother, father, and I were in Sag Harbor, Long Island for our vacation. Every August, we spent three weeks in Sag Harbor in a bungalow we rented for $75.00 a week. Almost every day my father would take his outboard motor to the dock where he rented a rowboat to go out into the bay to fish. He left around 6:00 am and didn't return until 5:00 pm. My mother took me to the beach in the afternoon. One day, when my father wasn't fishing, the manager of the company from whom we rented the bungalow came by with a note for my father to call his cousin, Charlie. We all knew that the call meant my grandfather had died. My grandfather, whom I had met only once, had called for my father several months earlier. He was dying of cancer, and he wanted my father to come to see him so he could ask my father for his forgiveness for the beatings. My father refused to go.

Since we had no phone in the bungalow, we went to a small restaurant at the beach where my mother took me to swim. The two-lane macadam road separated the restaurant from the beach. It was a typical beach shack that served food. If I remember correctly, that was its name—the Beach Shack. The wooden rectangular building was built on wooden stilts to protect it from the onslaught of high surf during hurricanes that seldom came to Long Island. We climbed up the gray, unpainted, weather-beaten stairs. The entrance led to a small alcove where the black pay phone hung on the wall to our left. At the front of this one-room restaurant was the soda fountain and grill where patrons could get hamburgers, hot dogs, and vanilla ice cream cones with chocolate sprinkles. A row of booths hugged each side of the room by the windows while two rows of booths divided the room in half. At each booth was a small jukebox. We took the booth nearest the front by the window. On most days, my mother would give me a quarter and I could select five songs to listen to while we ate. But today there was no quarter. There was no talking, either. We all knew that my grandfather was dead. My father hated his father, so why bother with the call, I thought, let's just get out of here. I squirmed in my seat and played with the levers on the jukebox, looking at the titles of all the songs. The building creaked as the wind blew against it. I watched my father go back to the alcove to make the call to Charlie. I forget how long he was gone and I forget if we ever had anything to eat. I saw my father come back. I was frightened. I had never seen him look this way before. From what I remember, his dark, tanned face had turned red. His jaw was rigid and his skin taut. He said nothing.

"Are you going to the funeral?" my mother asked.

"No."

At that moment, our roles reversed. My father looked so hurt that I wanted to tell him that I loved him and wanted him to be my father more than anyone else, and that I would never let anything come between us like it did with him and his father. But I didn't know how to say those words. How can a nine-year old be a father to his father? I did the only thing I knew. I secretly promised my father that I would never let him die alone.

As it turned out, I couldn't be with my father at the time of his death. He had fallen and hit his head hard against the pavement. From what my stepmother told me, his Alzheimer's progressed rapidly and he became belligerent and confused in the hospital. He refused to eat. She called and said that the hospital wanted to put a feeding tube into his stomach. I told her under no circumstances should she do that. My years of experience as a pastor had shown me that when people refuse to eat it usually means they want to die. My father also had told me when I saw him last, that he wanted to die. Yet, as I spoke authoritatively to my stepmother, I realized I was signing my father's death warrant. I knew it was what he wanted, but I also felt guilty, because part of me wanted him to die, too. We had just begun our life as father and son and we needed more time, but it came too late. His passing would mean that while I would have to face reality and live with the fact that I didn't have the father I wanted, my struggle would be over. Yet, I also thought my feelings might be God's way of telling me that it was time to let go and trust God to redeem our relationship. I couldn't fulfill my promise to my father, but by conducting his funeral I could, at least, lay him to rest and help him to get home, safely.

3

Beauty and the Beast

Everyone is haunted by their past.
Russell Crowe
as John Nash in *A Beautiful Mind*

If Hugh Hefner had started publishing Playboy in 1930 instead of 1953, my mother could have been his first Playmate, although such a thought would have been revolting to her. Born Sadie Black, but called Sally or Sis, on August 7, 1910, in her home at 508 6th Avenue in Brooklyn, New York, she was the last of four children and the only girl. She was a petite woman, 5'1", with naturally blond hair and blue eyes. She had a figure at the age of eighteen that I would guess was 34-25-34, which she kept mostly through her life. The golden waves of her shoulder length hair framed a bright, beaming, and infectious smile. She easily attracted attention wherever she went, especially from men. She told me that she sang and danced in Vaudeville with her brother, Bob, palled around with Mae West, and was discovered by a talent scout when she was nineteen who wanted to take her to Hollywood and get her into the movies, but her father forbade her leaving.

"Hollywood is no place for a young woman," he said.

"So, I didn't go," my mother told me. "But if I had gone, I wouldn't have had you."

She told me this story so many times that I got the impression she regretted obeying her father. She often said with a sense of sadness and grief that she did little for herself; she only did what others thought she should do. So, it didn't take much for me to think that I was her consolation prize, and that I was to be the one who would fulfill her life-long ambitions. From the moment I was conceived, I believe I was set up to fail as my mother's only son and child.

My parents met at Budd Lake, New Jersey, in 1930. My father was one of the boys in the band that was playing at the dance hall. My mother, along with friends, made weekly pilgrimages to New Jersey. She loved to dance and her beauty insured she would not be without a partner. During one of the intermissions, a mutual friend introduced them. To hear my mother talk about it, it was love at first sight.

"Your father didn't say much," she said.

"What attracted you to him?"

"He looked so handsome in his tux. And, boy, could he play the trumpet. When he played a solo, everyone stopped dancing and listened to him. I just knew he was the one for me."

My mother's natural talkativeness and my father's quiet demeanor allowed my mother to take center stage, and relieved my father of the responsibility of carrying a conversation. My mother liked the limelight and with my father, she had it both ways—she was the main performer in their relationship, and she could hold court at the dance hall as the girlfriend of a band member with those wishing to be close to celebrity.

On March 15, 1931, my parents married. The characteristic that had attracted my mother to my father was what attracted other women to him—the desire to be in the limelight and associate with a celebrity, even though he was a consummate introvert. There is something seductive about a man on stage as my mother found out. Early in their marriage, she discovered she shared her husband with other women.

It was in the midst of this infidelity that I was conceived in February, 1941. I don't know why my parents waited ten years to have a child. As I studied marriage counseling later in my life, I found that couples waiting that long to have a child, unless it is due to a physical condition that prevents conception or some other serious extenuating circumstance, often have serious conflicts within the marriage. It shows an inability to make an important decision. If a couple cannot agree to have a child, they're probably not agreeing on many other issues either. Maybe my parents thought a child would bring them closer together. If anything, my birth marked the onset of more disruption.

Six weeks after I was born, the Japanese attacked Pearl Harbor, the United States entered World War II, and gasoline and food became scarce.

To my parents, those concerns were minor compared to the fact that my father almost died from spinal meningitis.

"He was playing in the Broadway show, *Best Foot Forward*," my mother said. "We think some of the soldiers who came to the play brought the germ with them. He came home one night vomiting with a high fever. How he drove home, I don't know. He was delirious and at the hospital, they had to tie him down to keep him in bed. His parents came to help Mom (my grandmother, Nana) and me take care of him. They also paid the hospital bill."

After a long hospital stay, he slowly recovered but then was plagued with severe headaches, on a regular basis, for the rest of his life. My parents must have overcome this disruption because my mother became pregnant again. However, the conception lodged in one of her fallopian tubes causing her to abort and requiring an extended hospital stay of her own. They didn't try again.

I remember wondering, as I was growing up, what my brother or sister would have been like. I wished I had someone with whom to share the burden of being in this family. My father was distant, my mother's moods were unpredictable, and my grandmother, who lived with us, was often cranky. Had I had a brother or sister, I wouldn't have been the only one to get yelled at, nor be the lone child in this adult community.

I was a good boy and the son every parent wished for. According to the Myers-Briggs Type Indicator® (MBTI®) I am an INFJ. The MBTI® is a personality questionnaire developed by Isabel Briggs and her mother, Katherine Myers, based on the personality theory of the late Swiss psychiatrist, Carl Jung. It has been translated into over sixty languages, and is used by many Fortune 500 companies to help build teamwork and understanding among employees. As an INFJ, I am an introverted intuitive feeler who likes a scheduled life. Less than two percent of the population is INFJ, which means that most people misunderstand us. My greatest strength is my intuition. Intuitive people look at the big picture. We often miss the details because we are more interested in the ambiance of a situation. Coming home from a dinner party at a friend's house my wife might remark, "Wasn't that a beautiful picture over their mantle piece." To which I might reply, "What picture, what mantel piece?" In addition, my intuition is introverted, which means you will not see what I see unless I choose to reveal it to you, and my selection of those to whom I reveal myself is limited. I must be able to trust you.

However, the function I use to greet others is my extroverted feeling. Extroverted feelers are warm, caring people. If you were to meet me in person, you would notice that my first concern is you. My words would be warm and my handshake firm, with my left hand probably embracing your elbow. Many people have walked away from conversations with me thinking that I agreed with them when, in fact, I had not. It was just that I thought it was more important to listen to their opinion than to express mine. Extroverted feelers want to please others. We usually dress well because we are not only dressing for ourselves but for others. As children, we want to please adults, especially our parents. As we reach out in love, we hope that love will be returned. When it is not, we are devastated, and we doubt our ability to be loved, especially by God. Likewise, we trust instinctively and when that trust is broken, we hurt deeply. In adulthood, other men look upon a feeling male with suspicion. Men are not supposed to be feeling, that's what women are for. We relate better to women than to men, which sometimes causes men to wonder about our intentions with their women. The downside of being an extroverted feeler is the difficulty we have of saying, *No*, or in standing up for ourselves. If we are not careful, people will take advantage of us. Another danger is that since we are so eager to please, we may never do the things we want to do.

I was also the perfect student. Early in the second grade, and before the incident below, the principal of the Glen Cove Elementary School, a woman, put her arm around me and gave me a hug. She said, "You're a joy to have at school, Walter. Your mother is fortunate to have a son like you, and you are fortunate to have a mother like her." I was the good boy who never got into any trouble, at least not much, but when I did, my mother would make sure that I knew the consequences of straying too far from the mold she had cast for me. I was taught early in life that I should behave, not just for my own good, but because my actions would be a reflection on my mother's reputation. She enjoyed the honor that came with being known as the mother of a good boy. It validated her role as a mother and gave her hope that I was not going to end up like her unfaithful husband. However, on at least one occasion that hope was threatened.

Miss Woodbury was my teacher in the second grade. I didn't like her. She wasn't a warm person. Her speech was curt, lacked emotion, and she didn't give me much attention. It was an early October day, the leaves were turning their brilliant colors, and the sunny air was clean and crisp. I went up to Miss Woodbury's desk.

"Miss Woodbury, when do we get out for Christmas vacation?"

"I don't know, Walter. Why do you ask?"

"I don't like school."

"Walter, that's an awful thing to say."

And I guess it was. My mother worked at The Little Shop, a baby store in downtown Glen Cove. When she came home from work that night, I was upstairs in my room. I went to my room as soon as I came home from school in somewhat of a self-imposed exile. I fidgeted with one thing after another as I anxiously waited for my mother to come home for I instinctively knew someone would have told her what I said. I heard the door open and then slam shut with a thud that shook the house.

"Get the hell down here," she shouted up the stairs.

I came down not knowing what my mother was going to do, but I did know it would be painful, and I would be unable to prevent it.

"What do you mean telling your teacher you don't like school?"

"I don't," I said.

"Do you realize how embarrassed I felt when your teacher came to the store today and told me what you said? Everyone in town knows what you said and they think it is just disgusting."

One thing about my mother was that she didn't lie. For the next several days, adults told me how I should like school and should never say anything like that because it hurt my mother.

"People think I'm a bad mother," she continued. "You don't give a damn about me. Don't you ever say anything like that again."

I started to cry. "I'm sorry," I said through my sobs.

"You're not sorry, you little snot."

"Yes, I am." I pleaded, but I couldn't convince her. She walked away from me. I followed her sobbing, "I'm sorry, Mom."

"Get out of my sight."

For the next four or five days, my mother didn't speak to me. She didn't say "good morning" or "hello" when she came home from work. She walked past me as if I didn't exist. My grandmother always got me ready for school and made my breakfast and lunch, but when my mother wasn't talking to me, it felt like my grandmother was my punishment. I wasn't good enough to be cared for by my mother, so she called in another woman. There were no belts, cat-o-nine tails, paddles, or canes in our home with which my mother could beat my bare bottom—only the lashes of her tongue, and then what seemed to be endless days of silence when I didn't exist in my mother's eyes. This was how she punished me and would punish me throughout my life. The effects were devastating. I felt worthless. I began to think I didn't exist. I wondered if this was what the wrath of God was like. Would God stop talking to me if I didn't please him? Would God deny my existence, too? As I look back on it now, this was the seed of my doubting not only my own worth, but my worth before God.

There were a lot of rewards for being a good boy and an only child, however. My mother, who lived through the Great Depression, always said, "You're going to have what your father and I never had." I took that as a sign that she and my father loved me, and I was never disappointed with the gifts they bestowed on me, especially at Christmas.

Christmas was always a joyful time around our house. Whatever problems the family had, Christmas was the time to put them away and enjoy one another; something like "R and R" for a soldier in the midst of a war. My grandmother stopped complaining about my father, my father was unusually talkative, and the tirade my mother was on the week before evaporated. Christmas was a holiday for us not in the sense of celebrating Christ's birth, but in the sense of taking time off from our lives to claim that which we wished we had during the rest of the year.

My father, for whom Christmas was the best part of the year, took pleasure in buying high quality gifts for my mother and me. He let my mother buy the gifts for my grandmother. Over the years, I received a short wave radio, portable television, motion picture projector, tape recorder, pool table, camera equipment, and whatever else I expressed a desire to have. Considering this was the 1950s, the gifts were extraordinary, and I had the pleasure of showing them off to the neighborhood kids making them wish they had parents like mine. There was also the annual admiration of the gifts received from Guy Lombardo: a twenty-five pound smoked turkey, which I loved, and four bottles of high quality scotch, gin, vodka, and bourbon. While I could not indulge in the liquor, I admired the shape and color of the bottles.

"Christmas wouldn't be Christmas without my Pink Ladies," my mother announced a few days before Christmas hinting to my father that she wanted him to make her up a pitcher of Pink Ladies, which he did willingly. A Pink Lady is a creamy pink cocktail made of gin, grenadine syrup, light cream, and eggs whites served in a martini glass. On Christmas Day, she would always have one in her hand, sipping it slowly and telling me how much she loved me.

"We've got our problems, Butch," as she called me. "But we love each other, and we'll get through." Usually, this was said with my father nearby, and in a rare display of affection, the three of us would have a group hug while our Airedale, Taffy, feeling left out would start barking and jumping up on us causing us to laugh. We put our arms around Taffy as she stood on her hind legs, tail wagging, and licking our faces.

My grandmother was never included in these hugs; she was usually busy in the kitchen getting Christmas dinner ready. I don't think she would have joined in anyway considering her feelings toward my father. On second reflection, I don't remember her being invited. It was as if my parents were declaring that only the three of us were the family. I never experienced my parents alone without the presence of my grandmother with the exception of these annual hugs and the time we moved from New York to California. It was as if we never got to mature as a family or that my parents never got to grow up. When a wife always has her mother with her, it is hard to see herself as a mature woman, and it is hard for her husband to make love to his wife with his mother-in-law in the next room.

I felt cheated. The times I spent with my mother and father alone were good times. I often wondered if we would not have had better times if my Grandmother did not live with us. Maybe my parents would not have divorced if they lived on their own. I vowed early in my teen years never to have my mother or my future mother-in-law live with my family and me. What is more interesting is that my mother told me many times when I got to be an adult that she would never come to live with my wife and me. She said, "I wouldn't do that to you; I won't do to you what Mom did to me." And she didn't. When she got older and was less able to take care of herself, I suggested she come live with us. By this time, I felt secure enough as a person that I could handle my mother's presence without reverting to being her little boy. She refused again, citing her earlier pledge. In spite of all of our problems, I admire my mother for not wanting to inflict herself on my family. At the end of her life, she died alone in a nursing home after having taken care of her mother, who died at the age of ninety-eight, and an alcoholic brother who died at eighty-seven. She didn't give me the love I wanted, but she did give me my adulthood without her hovering presence.

As I look back on it, Christmas was not only a holiday from our family conflicts; it was also a confessional day that recognized that we were not living up to what we had hoped would be our lot in life. My mother's acknowledgement that we had problems but we would get through them was said with such sincerity and joy with her bright blue eyes looking directly into mine that I realized how much I loved her and how good it was to be with her. I also realized I was extremely attracted to my mother, and I hoped one day that my wife would be just like her.

Other people enjoyed her, too. They loved coming to parties at our house. My mother would flirt with the men and her stunning looks and figure led the men to reciprocate. She made everyone feel relaxed and valued. For many years, she worked as a sales woman for large department stores such as Lord and Taylor and Saks Fifth Avenue. She had a devoted clientele of women who only wanted her to wait on them, and if they came to the store on her day off, they would come back another day. One day, I was in Lord and Taylor's in Manhasset, New York when my mother was helping one of her loyal customers. The woman was trying on several outfits and after she would look at herself in the mirror, she would say:

"What do you think, Sally, how do I look?"

"I'll tell you, toots, it's not your color and it makes you look heavy around the hips." Those she liked, she always called *toots*.

"Thanks Sally, I know I can always depend on you for an honest answer."

After the woman left without purchasing anything, my mother's boss who had observed the interaction came over to my mother.

"Sally, why did you tell her she didn't look good in those clothes?"

"Because she didn't," my mother said.

"But we have to make sales. That's why we're in business."

"So what do you want me to do? I could have made the sale, but in three or four days the woman would have return the clothes and what good would that have done you?"

At that point, my mother's boss walked away. She knew my mother was right because my mother had the fewest returns of merchandise she sold of any salesperson in the store. Her boss also knew that when that woman came back, and they did have clothes that suited her, she would make a large purchase.

∽

When we moved to Glen Cove in 1947, I was five and didn't know I was a part of an historical movement. World War II had ended and the suburbs had their beginning. The suburbs brought with them the hope that we would all live happily ever after as long as a family had a husband, wife, and two children, preferably a boy first and a girl second, and a station wagon in the garage. My parents had one child, one car but no station wagon, and no garage. Were we not part of the American dream? A few months after moving to Glen Cove, I overheard my mother say to my grandmother, "I gotta get out of here. I gotta find a job. Staying home is driving me crazy." I took this to mean she didn't want to be around me. She was leaving because I was not a good son. Why is she turning her job as a mother over to her mother? I felt abandoned.

My mother got a job at the Little Shop, a baby store. She loved the work. She talked so much about how cute babies were that I began to feel that what was wrong with me was that I was not a baby anymore. Was my mother secretly wishing I was still a baby?

The Little Shop was owned, if I remember correctly, by a Robert Little, who used his last name to identify the purpose of his enterprise. My mother thought he was a "jerk." "He doesn't know his ass from a hole in the ground when it comes to running the business," she often said. As the years went by, I heard her say the same about all of her male bosses. Was there something about an adult male that she didn't like; something that made her uncomfortable, and upon whom she projected her inner conflicts on all men?

I remember one day when I was about eleven. It was early morning and I went into my parent's bedroom and climbed into bed with my mother. My parents slept in single beds divided by two nightstands. At the end of each bed, they had their own chest of drawers. I didn't think anything of it at the time because when I watched, *I Love Lucy* I saw that Lucy and Ricky had separate beds. On this particular morning my father was getting dressed. He took his pajamas off and was nude.

"God, look at that small peter," my mother said, laughing. "Have you ever seen anything so small? And those balls aren't much either." We laughed at my naked father. He dressed quickly and left the room without saying a word.

That memory haunts me to this day. I cringe when I think of what my father felt that morning having his manhood laughed at. I also cringe when I think of what my mother thought of my small *peter* and balls. If my mother could laugh at my father, she could laugh at me. What, then, might other women think when they saw me naked? I began to develop a fear of revealing too much of myself to others; afraid I would be laughed at. As an intuitive, I have many ideas that often seem farfetched to others so I keep many of my thoughts to myself not wanting the exposure. Nakedness is not only physical, it's also emotional. That day in my parent's bedroom, the two dimensions coalesced into a single reality. Revealing too many of my ideas would be equivalent to standing nude in front of others and being ridiculed.

There were times, however, when I felt validated by my mother, when she showed me a side of herself that made me proud, and I felt safe in a world that I didn't understand. I had a new friend in the third grade. His name was Alexander. I forget his last name. He was a Negro, as we called African-Americans in those days. His mother was a nurse. She was tall, slender, had a loving face, and looked beautiful in her uniform. One day, she had taken Alexander and me on an outing. I forget where we went, but we came back sweaty and dirty. She told us to take a shower. I was embarrassed to strip in front of her, but she turned her back to us and we stripped and took our showers. She just knew to respect our privacy, and I loved her for that. Alexander and I, on other days, would come home to my house after school with our arms wrapped around each other. We laughed and talked, but I can't remember what about. I overheard my grandmother tell my mother when she came home from work one night:

"Sis, some of the neighbors told me they don't like Walter coming home with his arms wrapped around a Negro. They don't like those kinds of people in our neighborhood, they said."

"One came into the store today and told me the same thing, Mom. I told her to go to hell. My son can have whoever he wants as a friend, and, besides, Negroes are no better or worse than we are."

I knew Alexander's skin was a different in color than mine, yet I couldn't understand why the neighbors were upset. But, I was proud my mother stood up for me, and prouder still that she saw my friend as a valid human being.

It was difficult to reconcile the loving side of my mother's nature, especially at Christmas, and her sense of social justice, with her unpredictable outbursts of rage followed by her stony silence and her disrespect for men. Being a "good boy," in her eyes, meant that I did exactly what she wanted me to do. Did her father's refusing to let her go to Hollywood and possibly sexually abusing her (I will deal with this in chapter 8), and her unfaithful husband radically diminish her confidence in men? Did it create a need in her for a man she could count on—a man who would take away the sins of the other men in her life? Is that why she elected me to be that man?

My mother's need for a perfect man, in many respects, reflects the Christian doctrine of the atonement. There are many theories of the atonement but they all deal with how we are reconciled to God. One such theory suggests that God wants us to be perfect. Because we are not, no matter how hard we try, we are doomed to be sinful. This angers God and separates us from God. The way to close the gap between God and humans is to remove the separation. So God came to earth in the person of his son, Jesus Christ. Jesus was perfect in every way. He was perfect God and perfect man. God was so pleased with what Jesus did that when God looks at us, God sees Jesus Christ and forgives us. The separation between God and the people is closed. My mother's search for the perfect man was in some respects similar to God's search. She made only two mistakes—she forgot she wasn't God, and that I wasn't Jesus Christ.

4

The Jesus Nut

The Jesus Nut is a hexagonal nut that holds the rotor blades of a helicopter securely to the body of the helicopter. Those who repaired and flew helicopters coined the term during the Vietnam War. If the nut failed in flight, the rotor blades would detach from the helicopter causing it to crash, and the only thing the passengers could do was to pray to Jesus."

WIKIPEDIA, THE FREE ENCYCLOPEDIA

"Hi, Nana," I said as I came in the back door of our home at 30 Phillips Road in Glen Cove, New York. It was late June 1948. Our Cape Cod, red brick house with its two-dormer windows and black roof was in a new neighborhood. Many of the homes had yet to be occupied, and the houses beyond us were in the process of being built. Our backyard faced open woods where every now and then a donkey from a neighboring farm appeared and walked around the buildings as if he were inspecting them. I was just a few months shy of my seventh birthday. School had been out for two weeks, and I was beginning to enjoy the carefree days of summer. My grandmother was in the kitchen to the left of the door laying out the ingredients for our evening supper. My mother was at work at the Little Shop in downtown Glen Cove.

The kitchen was a small square area whose, one color, white, dominated its decor. A white porcelain sink with a window trimmed in white paint faced the backyard. A white porcelain gas stove occupied the center of the back wall, and a white metallic refrigerator was opposite the sink. In between these appliances, were white metal cabinets, both on the floor and above the white counter tops. To the right of the door was our dining room with an oval oak table covered by a red and white checked oilcloth, that was covered with a linen cloth for dinner, and surrounded by four oak armless, bow-back Windsor chairs with four additional chairs in the corners of the dining room.

There was a big hunk of red meat on the counter to the right of the sink along with potatoes, carrots, celery, and onions. "What's that?" I said, pointing to the meat.

"That's pot roast," my grandmother said. "I thought you were out playing with your friends."

"I was. We were playing cowboys and Indians but the cowboys shot all the Indians, and then Joey's mother called him to come in for lunch, and we all came home."

"Were you an Indian or a cowboy?"

"I was an Indian. I was that yesterday, too. But yesterday we shot all the cowboys."

"I guess you're even."

"Can I have a peanut butter and jelly sandwich?" I said.

"Sure." My Grandmother pulled out the loaf of soft white bread, a jar of Skippy Peanut Butter and Welch's grape jelly, and made me my sandwich. She also poured me a glass of milk and brought over the package of Oreo cookies for my dessert. She poured a glass of milk for herself, too, sat down at the dining room table with me, and dunked several Oreo cookies in the milk, consuming them while I ate my sandwich.

When I finished my lunch, I got up and gave her a hug and a kiss. "Thanks, Nana, I love you," I said, and then ran upstairs to my room to play with my dolls, Barbara and Sally. Sally was named for my mother. I don't remember what led me to give the other doll her name except that I liked saying the word, *Barbara.*

When I first met my grandmother, she was fifty-nine years old, and her 5'4" frame supported 230 pounds, which came mostly from her insatiable appetite for Italian food and sweets, especially chocolates. Boxes of Whitman's and Fanny Farmer candies decorated the house and were treated as one would treat a rare artifact. An excellent cook, she did all the cooking for our family. But as I look back on it now, I cringe when I think of all the artery-clogging foods she fed us. Mashed potatoes with gravy, corn, peas and other vegetables, along with bread and real butter (margarine was only for poor people, in her opinion) were the natural partners of whatever meat she was cooking, and eggs were fried in the grease left over from the cooked bacon. She labored a good part of the day in the kitchen, and at night served the evening meal on a formal dining room table often with a linen tablecloth and napkins, serving bowls for each of the vegetables, and a platter for the meat. I learned the art of dining at an early age.

In the fall of 1948, I entered the second grade—a year I will never forget. Nana determined that I needed a good breakfast to "stay with me through the day." Every morning she made me oatmeal. I can remember clearly the picture of the long white-haired Quaker with a black hat on the round red, white, and blue cardboard carton of Quaker Oats greeting me as I came into the kitchen each morning. Our milk came in quart-sized glass bottles that had a layer of cream on top, and Nana made sure I got a good portion of the cream on my oatmeal. I hated it. The cream seemed to make the oatmeal thicker; it was like eating play dough. Years later, I found out I had milk allergy and probably had it since I was a child, which would account for why it seemed so thick and indigestible. To this day, I cannot bring myself to eat oatmeal or drink milk.

I never complained to Nana about the oatmeal; I was programmed to keep my feelings to myself. On the other hand, it represented love and security. Every morning I came down from my bedroom, my grandmother would be dressed and cooking my breakfast. She was always there. It wasn't my mother who made sure I was sent off to school in good condition, it was Nana. Nana was there at the door when I came home from school, had cookies and milk ready for me, and fed me again at dinner. When I came home crying with my knees bloodied from a fall, it was Nana who took me into the bathroom, gently cleaned my wounds, bandaged them, gave me a kiss, and sent me back out to play. She was also my protector and I felt safe with her especially when my mother had a tantrum about something I had done. Nana would say, "Leave the poor kid alone," and my mother would quiet herself down. I always felt that Nana was on my side; that we were facing the world together.

During that summer, my father drove Nana and me to downtown Glen Cove to go shopping. We stopped at the Little Shop to see my mother who was holding a baby in her arms, telling the baby's mother what a cute little girl she had, and suggesting different kinds of clothing for the child. We then went to a jewelry store where I spotted a wristwatch that was silver and had a shiny black leather band. It was the most beautiful watch I had ever seen in my life.

"Oh, Nana, can I have this watch," I said.

"How much is it, Mr. Williams?" she said to the storeowner. I think that was his name.

"That's $8.00, Mrs. Black." Glen Cove was a small town in 1948 and everyone knew each other.

"Oh, Walter, I don't have that much money."

"But Nana, I really want it."

"Well, let's see if I can save up for it."

At the time, she had little savings, and her only income was $50.00 a month from my grandfather's pensions for having served in the Navy and the New York Fire Department. She was giving about half of that to my mother and father for household expenses. But every month she'd set aside two dollars for my watch. I kept asking her how soon she would have all the money and was always disappointed when she replied, "another month or two."

Two days before my birthday on October 26, she said, "Walter, for your birthday, I'm going to get you the watch."

"Really, oh Nana, I love you," I said as I threw my arms around her large torso and kissed her repeatedly. On the day of my birthday, she took me back to the jewelry store.

"Hello, Mrs. Black," Mr. Williams said.

"Hello, Mr. Williams. I'm here to buy my grandson that watch, if you still have it. Today's his birthday."

"Well, Happy Birthday, young man. How old are you?"

"I'm seven."

"Well, let's get the watch for you. That's a mighty fine watch, Mrs. Black. He must be a good grandson."

"He's the best."

Mr. Williams took the watch out of the box and put it on my wrist. "Now you take good care of this watch, young man. Your grandmother loves you very much."

"Oh, yes sir," I said. Now I can be like my Dad, I thought. I had watched him take off and put on his watch many times wondering if I would ever be old enough to have one of my own. What was even better was that I was the first among my friends to have one. Every night I went to bed, I put it back in its box and laid it on my nightstand.

∼

Born Sadie Spencer on July 29, 1882, in Brooklyn, New York, Nana was the oldest of seven children, six from the marriage of her father, Victor Emmanuel Spencer and his wife, Ann Hull, and one from Ann's second marriage. Her father emigrated from Sweden and worked at Ellis Island processing new immigrants to the United States mainly because he could speak five languages fluently. An alcoholic, he spent most of the family's money on his drinking addiction. Ann divorced him in the late 1890's, leaving her with four girls and two boys to raise on the little income she received from taking in washing and ironing, and forcing my grandmother to go to work at age fifteen to help support the family. Nana's four sisters were: Lillian who died of breast cancer in 1956, Mabel who scared me to death telling me that God was going to destroy the world with fire and earthquakes soon, Barbara who died in her early 30's, and the youngest, Estelle, who was born in 1898 and lived most of her life in Chicago. Her two brothers were Dewit and LeRoy, called Roy, and of whom she often spoke. Dewit died before I was born.

"Roy wanted to be a minister," she told me many times, as I was growing up. "But then he was in the Army in WWI, was gassed, and came back shell-shocked."

I never met Roy, but a few weeks after I was ordained a Presbyterian minister in 1967, I talked to him by telephone. He was about seventy-five years old.

"I'm proud of you, Walter," he said. "I always wanted to be a minister, but after what I saw in the war, I couldn't believe anymore. I never knew people could do things like that to others. I can't understand why God would allow such things to happen."

"Maybe God didn't let it happen, Uncle Roy."

"You're probably right, but for me, it's too late. But, it's not too late for you. Pray for me."

∼

My grandmother came to live with my mother, her daughter, and her new son-in-law in 1931, shortly after my parents were married and her husband, John Black, died of stomach cancer. She remained with my mother until she died a few months before her ninety-ninth birthday in 1981.

Black was my grandmother's second husband. Her first husband, Jerry Richards, owned a razor blade factory where my grandmother worked and was about four years older than she was. One day, she collapsed at work, and Richards took her home and summoned the doctor who discovered she was severely malnourished and mentally and physically exhausted. I'm sure the recent divorce of her parents and the alcoholism of her father helped create her condition. My mother told me that my grandmother was embarrassed when Richards brought her home and saw the squalor in which she lived with her mother and siblings. He also discovered that they only had bread and coffee to eat and drink. Richards began supplying the family with food, increased my grandmother's salary, which he paid while she recuperated, and visited her on a regular basis. A romance blossomed and they married six months later, which made my grandmother an instantly wealthy woman and the envy of her sisters.

It was an odd relationship because Richards was Jewish and my grandmother was fundamentalist Baptist. His family was opposed to the marriage and never welcomed my grandmother into their home. However, from what I heard, she loved him and they had two sons, Sidney and Matthew or Matty as he was called. The two boys didn't look like brothers. Sydney was six feet tall, debonair, a sharp dresser who lived in San Diego, California in his adult years, and was financially successful most of his life from what I remember. Matty was 5'3" tall, a mechanic and an alcoholic, and lived most of his life in Irving, Texas in poverty.

In his mid-twenties, Richards developed Tuberculosis, or consumption as it was called in the early 1900s, and he and my grandmother went by steamship to Germany for treatment. She told me there was a sanitarium in Germany (she didn't identify the city or the institution) that she and her husband heard had the best and latest treatment for Tuberculosis. However, the doctors there told him that his condition had progressed to the point where they couldn't help him. He died at the age of twenty-eight, in 1906, shortly after they returned from Germany.

My grandmother opened a candy and ice cream store from the money she received as her inheritance from her deceased husband. She hired her sisters to help her with the store since they were poor, but the infighting between the sisters and their jealousy of their wealthy older sister made them ineffective workers and my grandmother ended up doing most of the work while financially supporting the family and her sons. That wasn't the only problem my grandmother was facing. Soon after her husband's death, she was beset by lawsuits from Richard's family claiming she had no right to his inheritance. "No sooner would one lawsuit end in my favor than another one would come along. I lost everything even though I won all the suits," Nana told me. "The ones who made money were the lawyers."

During the time she had the candy store, a firefighter with the New York Fire Department, John Black, came into the store. His 5'10" body was lean and strong according to my mother. He parted his fine, dark brown hair on the left, combed it to the right, and let it lie flat on his narrow oval-shaped head with the hair on the side cut close to the scalp. He had what barbers call a straight up cut. A picture of him in 1926 at the Elks Clam Bake shows him with a dark suit, long-sleeve white shirt, dark bow tie, and white socks. "He always wore white socks," my mother said. "It came from his Navy days." My grandmother and he had known each other since childhood when they went to grammar school together. According to my mother, my grandmother said when he walked into the store:

"What are you doing here?"

"I saw your sister, Mabel, in the bar and she told me to come see you."

Mabel was a regular at the bars in Brooklyn and never looked away from any man who paid attention to her. By the time she died in the 1970s, she had had three husbands, all of whom died, and the family was never sure if she had married her last husband.

Black was attracted to my grandmother but the feeling wasn't mutual. However, they were married, I believe, in 1908.

"I don't know why I married him, but I did," my grandmother told my mother later in her life.

"Did she love him?" I asked my mother.

"No."

"Did Black love her?"

"Oh, yes."

"Did she love Richards?" I asked.

"Very much. He took good care of her."

"Why do you think she married your father?"

"I think she was lonely and she had two boys to support."

When I think about it, she must have felt that life had given her an unfair and heavy burden, and that she saw in Black a man who could take responsibility and probably relieve her of some of her own. In addition to her alcoholic father, she was only twenty-four when she became a widow. She hardly had time to grieve over the death of Richards who probably filled the role of the good father for her, which made her love him even more and left a big void in her life when he died. After his death, she opened a business, dealt with lawsuits, and married a new man all within a span of two years. She soon had two more children, James in 1908, whom they called Bob or Dick, and Sadie, my mother, in 1910.

∼

Much of what I know about my grandfather comes from my mother. My grandmother said little about him and only halfheartedly agreed whenever my mother would praise her father to me when I was growing up. While my grandfather was a firefighter and liked his job, his first love was the Navy. He would have preferred a career in the Navy, but as he told my mother, he would always be gone and he had a family to support.

Black served in the Navy during the Spanish America War and WWI. My grandmother contends he was in the Philippines under Admiral Dewey. However, a search of the records of the ships under Dewey doesn't show his name. I have part of his naval record that shows him aboard the USS New York, the flagship of Admiral Sampson, that was part of the Naval forces that saw combat in the Battle of Santiago. The record shows him being on the ship from 1901 to 1902 when it toured Southeast Asia, Vladivostok, Russia, and Korea. He also served again on active duty in the Navy from May 14, 1918, to February 8, 1919. He was Honorably Discharged from the US Naval Reserves on April 17, 1922.

My grandfather became a Probationary Fireman at Engine Company 103 at 533 Hicks Street in Brooklyn, at an annual salary of $800.00 on July 10, 1906. In addition to fighting fires, he was responsible for taking care of the horses, which meant brushing and feeding them on a daily basis, polishing their harnesses, and training the Dalmatians to keep the horses quiet while they were at the scene of a fire. He loved animals and was always bringing a stray dog home to feed. During WWI, he saw a boatload of horses torpedoed by the Germans and sunk. He told my mother, "I cried for a week after seeing those horses die."

I know little of my grandfather's family except that they were Christian Scientists, and his parents separated when he was young. His mother died soon after the separation leaving an aunt to raise him and his two brothers.

"The family was strange and distant," my mother said, "At Papa's funeral only one of his brothers came."

Apparently, my grandfather was also a man about town. "He would leave in the morning for his shift at the Fire Department, and not get home until two or three o'clock the following morning," my mother said. "But he was always bringing sandwiches home. Mom liked the club sandwiches from the Elks Club the best."

"Papa was a no-nonsense type of father," my mother continued. "One time, the police caught my brother, Bob, riding on top of the trolley car—he was always getting into trouble. One of the police officers told my father they had him at the police station. My father said, 'Good, keep him overnight.' My mother was furious with Papa, but he didn't care. On another occasion, my brother Sidney ran away from home at seventeen. Papa said, 'if he wants to go, let him go,' and did nothing to find him. A few months later, Sidney wrote for money to come home which he sent to him and accepted him back into the family, although not with great fanfare."

My mother told me that after the United States entered WWI in 1917, my grandfather came home one evening and announced he had re-enlisted in the Navy. "He never asked us or gave us any indication he would re-enlist," she said. "Soon after he shipped out, he was reported wounded (although that remains uncertain) and then was reported as missing. For a year, we didn't know where he was, and the Navy refused to send Mom his salary. She had a three-karat diamond ring Richards gave to her on their engagement. She took the ring to my father's family and they loaned her money using the ring as collateral. When my grandfather came home, the Navy paid him his salary for the past year in full. My mother went back to the Black family to get the ring, but they had sold it. She was depressed for a long time after that."

∼

The more I got to know Nana, the more I realized she was a recluse. She never dated after the death of her second husband and she had no friends her own age. All her energies seemed to be devoted to keeping house for her daughter, son-in-law, and grandson, and she only left the house to take me for a walk when I was a toddler, to go shopping for clothing, and when our family would go out to dinner sometimes on Sundays. My father did most of the grocery shopping since Nana never learned to drive a car. Yet the impression I had of my grandmother as a young women was that she was outgoing. Her marriage to Richards, a wealthy businessman, owning and running her own business, and her marriage to my grandfather who was always having parties at the house led me to think she was different in her younger years. However, my mother told me she was never outgoing. She didn't make friends because she didn't need to do so—her sisters were around most of the time, and she didn't like going to social events with her husband. As I reflect on what I know about her early years, I surmise my grandmother never had a chance to develop her own personality before the forces of the world directed the course of her life. Without knowing who she was, how could she offer herself in friendship to another?

In the summer of 1949, I was in the basement with Nana as she was washing clothes. Our washing machine was one of the first automatic washers on the market; a white round metal tub set on four legs with small black wheels. Attached to the top of the tub was a swivel wringer composed of what looked like two rolling pins held together by a white metal frame. The washer agitated the clothes, emptied the soapy water into a large gray metal sink, refilled the tub with clean water, and rinsed the clothes. My grandmother then put the clothes through the wringer to squish out the remaining water. I was standing by the washer looking over the top entranced by its inner workings when she started putting the clothes through the wringer.

"Why do you need to do that, Nana?"

"So they can dry faster on the clothesline. Otherwise, it might take two or three days for them to dry. You don't want to wait that long for your underwear, do you?"

"Nope." I was enjoying this time with my grandmother so I was not prepared for what she said next.

"Walter, promise me that if anything happens between your mother and father you will always stay with your mother for she is the one who loves you, not your father."

What? I thought. My father doesn't love me? This short statement created shock waves inside me as if earthquakes were going off all over my body. I already doubted my father's love because he hardly talked to me, and now I was getting the confirmation that he really didn't love me. I thought I must be an awful person if my own father doesn't love me. If he can't love me, who can? I felt I was drifting alone in the world as if there was no one or no thing around that I could grasp to steady myself as the ground quickly shifted under my feet. No sooner had the first set of quakes ripped through my body, when the aftershocks came with as great of a force. I had no idea at this age that there was any trouble with my parents' relationship. I thought they would always be together. Were they going to split up? I thought. I was scared. Who would take care of me? I don't know how to take care of myself? How will I get a job? How will I survive?

I don't remember saying anything to my grandmother, although I probably mumbled something. That's what usually happens to me when I'm shocked—I become quiet and ponder what has taken place and what it might mean. What I do remember is hating my grandmother. I felt betrayed. I thought it was Nana and I against the world, but now I saw that it was Nana and my mother who were in a conspiracy together against my father and I was the battleground.

The fact that Nana was always home gave her an advantage in our family that neither my mother, father, nor I had. She was like a catcher on a baseball team. The catcher is the only member of the team who sees the entire field of play and has each player facing him with the exception of the batter. Since he is behind the batter, he can read his body language and judge the batter's next move. As a result, he determines the type of ball the pitcher will pitch, and signals other members of the team as to what may happen. All of our interactions and conversations went through Nana, and we told Nana things that we didn't tell each other. We gave her a lot of power and she didn't hesitate to use it. I remember one incident that was played out in front of me when I was thirteen years-old that typifies a recurrent scenario in our house.

"Do you know what that no-good-for-nothing husband of yours did today?" she said as my mother walked through the door from work. My father had already left for work.

"Not now, Mom, I'm tired. It's been a long day," my mother said.

"That poor kid of yours," she was always calling me the poor kid, "came home from school today wanting to show his father what he did in school and Walter said, 'show it to me another time.' Then he went back to lying on the sofa and drinking another can of beer. He's the worst father I've ever seen."

"I don't know what I'm going to do with him, Mom. I can't get him to stop drinking, and I keep on telling him that he needs to spend more time with Walter. What can I do?"

"He also said you need to dust your brains out. He's never seen such a dizzy blonde in all of his life."

At this point, my grandmother had successfully made my mother angry. My mother said, "Well, I'll tell that bastard a thing or two when I see him."

The next day, I came home from school and went to my room, but I could hear my grandmother talking to my father.

"Walter, you need to know that Sis is really pissed with you for not spending more time with the kid."

"What does she have to be pissed about? I'm going to take him to New York with me next week when I get fitted for my new tuxedos. I can't satisfy her. I got the house in Port Washington redecorated the way she wanted it, and then she says, 'I don't like this house, I want to move.' The same will probably happen with this house in a year or two. What can I do?"

"Well, you're right. She's never satisfied. She's been that way since she was a kid. At times, her father would wonder where her brains were; she never understood much of anything anyone told her."

I couldn't believe what I was hearing. My parents were having a fight over me and were doing it through my grandmother who was very happy to be the referee and steer the fight in the direction of her choosing. What was more amazing was that my grandmother took the side of the person with whom she was talking at the time, which effectively confirmed and reinforced the negative impressions my parents had of each other. The situation was made more poisonous by the fact that my parents never saw each other throughout the week. Sunday was the only day my father didn't have to work. During the week, he got home at 3:30AM and was asleep when my mother went to work at 8:30AM, and he left for work before she got home for supper. There was no time for them to talk, compare notes, or to understand what each was saying. Instead, their negative feelings for each other festered all week, so by the time Sunday came they walked about in icy silence only communicating when the situation demanded it. I realized that my grandmother was destroying my parent's marriage just as she tried to destroy my relationship with my father five years earlier. As I think about it now, what was worse was that my parents didn't seem to understand the dynamics of the situation; they didn't understand that my grandmother was directing how they should think and feel about each other.

As I went through my teenage years, I continued to love my grandmother and enjoy the many things she was always doing for me. She expanded the skills I acquired in cooking and sewing classes in eighth grade, taught me how to darn my socks, and iron my clothes. Knowing how to do such things came in handy when I was living on my own several years before I was married and didn't have money for new socks when holes appeared in the old ones. Throughout college, I used the set of *The Great Books of the Western World* she gave me for papers I had to write. She paid three hundred dollars for the books in 1957, and it took her a year to pay for them—nothing was too good for her grandson.

⁓

In 1956, my parents began thinking about moving from New York to Los Angeles. My mother was getting her "three-year itch," which is to say she tired of a house she lived in for more than three years. Each house she lived in was her dream house, but then the dream faded and a new dream had to take its place. For her the future was always more promising than the present. My father was also tired of working for Lombardo; he felt stuck in a profession that offered him no possibility for advancement. "There's no challenge to the music," he told me. "Any third-year music student could play what we play and we play the same songs every night."

My father was well connected to the music world on the west coast. He knew or worked with many of the show business people who were making a name for themselves such as Ray Conniff, Lawrence Welk, and Max Herman who was the Secretary-Treasurer of the Musicians Union. He phoned many of his friends and they all encouraged him to move to California. They told him the weather was great and with his musical talent, he wouldn't have any trouble getting work. I got excited about going to Los Angeles, or as I always called it, Hollywood, when I could see us having a house with a swimming pool and socializing with the movie stars with whom my father would work.

At the same time my parents were making their decision, California was conducting a media blitz to encourage people to move to the state or *The Land of Golden Opportunity*, as they called it. They showed people who had moved to California, set up new businesses, and now were wealthy with the luxury of going horseback riding every weekend or lying in the sun by their pool. They showed the beauty of the beaches, the fishing, hunting, and skiing opportunities, especially around Big Bear Lake in the San Bernardino Mountains. The ads virtually promised success, happiness, and wealth if you moved to California.

The decision to move to California was probably easy for my parents to make. In addition to the lure of the land was their dissatisfaction with their present circumstances, which also reflected their dissatisfaction with each other. About a year before they began thinking about moving, they had a big fight. It was a Sunday afternoon. The sun was bright and its rays were piercing the picture window of our living room that faced the west. My grandmother was in her usual chair and I was standing at the piano by the stairs. My parents bought me the piano six years earlier when I started taking piano lessons. My mother and father, for reasons unknown to me, were upstairs in my room with the door closed yelling at one another. The distance and the closed door made their words unintelligible. The noise quieted and after a few minutes of silence, my mother came down and announced, "We're getting a divorce." Neither she nor my father made any move to implement the divorce, but it was obvious the relationship was anything but good. They did what most couples do in similar circumstances; they looked to things external to heal themselves of their internal regrets and conflicts, and in California, they saw a way to start over and let the past remain in the east while the virgin future unfolded in the west.

My grandmother was not happy with the prospect of moving and she let my mother know of her displeasure after dinner one night when we were sitting in the living room.

"What the hell do you want to move for? Walter's making good money and you have the house of your dreams. You also have a son to think about. What happens if you get out there and Walter can't find work? How are you going to take care of the kid? And what's going to happen to me?"

"Well, we're going to move, Mom, whether you like it or not. You can either come or stay, it's up to you."

I think the prospect of my grandmother not making the move with us encouraged my parents. I overheard them one night after my grandmother had gone to bed.

"Do you think Tony and Florence would take her?" my father said. Florence was my grandmother's niece, the daughter of her sister Mabel.

"I already checked with them, Smitty," as she called my father. "They told me that they have their hands full with Mabel and their place is too small."

"Yeah, they are two peas in a pod all right. I wouldn't want the two of them either. But it would be nice to see what could happen in our marriage without your mother."

"We haven't had time for each other, have we? Everything we've done has been with Mom. Maybe things will be different in L.A."

My grandmother eventually agreed to the move. I don't remember what made her acquiesce except my parents' determination to move and realizing that at seventy-five she was too old to start living on her own.

Tony and Florence did agree that Nana could stay with them while we moved and settled into a house in LA. We took our cat, Fig, and our dog, Taffy, to our Vet, Dr. Berlinger. The plan was for him to keep them until we called. He would then put them on a plane, and send them to us traveling in the same cage. "They'll keep each other company and it won't be so fearful for them," he told us. They arrived in good shape, happy to see us, as we were to see them.

On Tuesday, August 6, 1957, after the last piece of furniture was secured on the moving van, we said our farewells to the neighbors, and with me in the back seat and my parents in the front, we left in our powder blue, four-door sedan 1954 Cadillac with white side-walled tires for what I later referred to as *The Great California Gold Rush of 1957*.

I don't remember much of the details of the trip. We drove straight through with few stops for sightseeing as we needed to meet the moving van and arrange for our furniture to go into storage. The Eisenhower Interstate System was still being constructed which meant that for part of the time we traveled uninterrupted at higher speeds, and at other times, we were reduced to two to three lane roads through numerous towns and cities. As we pulled out of our driveway at 9 Centre Drive in Roslyn, New York, the warm summer breeze blew across our faces through the open car windows.

"Well, we can't go back now, Smitty," my mother said.

"Who wants to go back?"

Not me, I thought. I sank my fifteen-year-old body comfortably into the back seat of the car as the tires moved effortlessly over the pavement, and I realized that for the near future my mother, father, and I were going to be together—Nana wasn't going to be with us. I wondered what it would be like. I didn't have to wait long to find out. My mother and father began to talk to each other and to me. Every so often one of us told a joke and all would laugh. My father had as one of his goals to spend a day in Las Vegas.

"I want you to see Vegas, Walter," he said. "There is nothing like it anywhere."

"Where are we going to stay there, Dad?"

"At Wilbur Clark's Desert Inn. Every time Lombardo came to Vegas we played there."

Clark built the Desert Inn and after several delays in construction for lack of money, it opened in 1950. It soon became famous for hosting PGA golf tournaments, and its most famous resident Howard Hughes who lived on the ninth floor and bought the hotel in 1966 for seven million dollars. The building was demolished in 2001 to make room for a new hotel.

"Do you know Wilbur Clark?"

"I met him once. He invited the band to his home for dinner one night. It was a big, beautiful house and there were cameras all over the property. He could see the goings and comings of everyone inside and outside his house any time he wanted. He had a twenty-five foot oval dining room table which was covered with all kinds of food—lobster, shrimp, caviar, steak, desserts, and anything you wanted to drink."

"Wow!" I said. "Why did he need the cameras?"

"Rumor had it that he was connected with organized crime. Those guys can play pretty rough. I would want to know who was coming to my house, too."

We arrived in Vegas around noon and checked into the Desert Inn. I wanted to go swimming and my mother went with me to the pool while my father went to the golf course to pick up a game. The temperature was 110 degrees. As soon as I took off my sneakers and felt the hot cement on my feet, I jumped in the water as fast as I could. The coolness of the water counteracted the heat of the sun, but my surprise as I got out of the water, I froze. I was shivering and I couldn't understand why I couldn't get warm in the blazing sun and the heat of the day. I thought I was sick. One of the employees saw me shivering.

"You know why you're so cold?" she said.

"No, I don't."

"The air is so dry and along with the heat, the water on your body is evaporating rapidly and is acting as a cooling agent. You'll be warm again in about ten minutes."

That evening we walked through the casino to the main restaurant. I was mesmerized with all the lights, and the noise from the slot machines going "ka ching" as coins were dropped in one after the other, and the arms on the machines not getting any rest as people hoped this next coin would result in the jackpot.

"Dad, can I play a slot machine?"

"You're too young, Walter. You have to be twenty-one to play. But I'll show you how it works."

We went over to a slot machine and my father dropped a quarter in, and when he went to pull the handle down, I pulled on his arm and felt the arm come to a sudden stop. He released the arm and the three spindles with their different drawings of fruit and other objects rolled round and round and came to a stop. Each spindle showed a different object meaning we didn't win anything. My father looked nervously around the room and then said to me, "I could get into a lot of trouble if some security officer saw you pull on my arm."

"Oh, I'm sorry."

"Hey Smitty, I just won ten bucks," my mother said from another slot machine. "How did you guys do?"

"We didn't win anything," my father said.

"You see it takes a woman's touch," my mother said.

My father chuckled and said to me, "Don't believe her. There's no such thing as 'a touch' when it comes to these one-arm bandits. The Casino sets them up so that they win far more often than the players do. I once saw a man put in two hundred silver dollars in one machine in one afternoon and didn't win anything. He left disgusted. Another man walked up to the same machine after he left, put a silver dollar in, and won a thousand dollar jackpot."

We passed the roulette tables and watched as the ball went round and round until in fell into the well and then into a numbered slot. The wheel master, as I think he was called, announced the number and its color, black or red, and with what appeared to be a small hockey stick in hand, raked in the chips that were not on the winning number or color.

"A few years ago, I saw Abbott and Costello lose $50,000 on the roulette table in one night," my father said. "It was their week's salary. I also got to know a couple in their sixties. The wife was so upset with her husband's gambling habits that she told him that he could only lose $5,000.00 a day. She was fed up with his losing $10,000 and more each day."

I couldn't imagine losing that much money, and when I think about it now that was 1950s dollars. Today those figures would easily be ten times what they were then.

We got to the restaurant and were seated at a round table that could accommodate six people. My father had called some of his friends and invited them to join us. The waiter gave us the menus, which were so tall that when I rested the bottom on my lap, the top came up to my nose.

"What should I get, Dad?"

"Get the prime rib, medium rare, and a baked potato with butter. You'll like it."

"You sure will," my mother said. "One thing about your father, I'll say, is that he knows how to eat well."

"Hey Walter, it's good to see you," a tall dark handsome man in his late forties greeted my father. "And Sally, you're as beautiful as ever," he said, as he leaned over and kissed my mother on the lips. Her right hand raised up and clasped him around the neck.

"Kenny, I want you to meet my son. Walter, this is Kenny Sergeant. We played with each other back in the 1930s."

Kenny extended his hand to me as I stood. I couldn't help but notice my mother looking affectionately at him as our hands clasped. So this was the Kenny Sergeant she had told me about on many occasions.

"Have a seat, Kenny," my father said. "Can you have dinner with us?"

"I would like to, but I have a show to do, but I have time for a drink." He ordered a scotch and soda, sat down at the table.

"So how is *old goosin butterflies*? Sergeant asked. *Old goosin butterflies* was the nickname musicians had given to Lombardo because instead of conducting the band while they played, he just danced around in front of them moving his white baton from the back to the front in a smooth semicircular motion that resembled a graceful goose.

"I'm glad to be out from under him," my father said.

"You're father's too good for Lombardo," Sergeant said to me. "And your mother is too good for your father. You don't how many hearts she broke when she married your dad, including mine. Not that your dad is bad, he's not. But your mother is so beautiful, everyone wanted to marry her."

"Oh Kenny, you're still a big flirt," my mother said chuckling. "Don't believe him, Walter, he's says that to all the women."

At this point, we were all laughing. My father was pleased to be praised by a colleague in front of his son, and my mother was happy to be back in the presence of a secret love. I was happy because I saw old friends enjoying their reunion, and because we were acting as I thought a family should.

My prime rib came. I was shocked. I never had a pound of meat for dinner before. It was an inch think and around the edges of the meat was red blood. It looked like the meat was a bright pink plateau of land that sharply dropped off into this red sea. Vegas must do everything big, I thought: big gambling debts, big casinos, big hunks of meat. After smothering my baked potato with butter, I cut into the prime rib and put a piece in my mouth. It felt smooth and soft as if it were caressing my inner cheeks. It offered no resistance to my teeth as they penetrated its silky fibers, and when it came time to swallow, it obediently entered the depths of my being.

Another man approached our table with a drink in his hand. By the way he walked, I could tell this was not his first drink of the evening.

"Hello, Walter, good to see you again. I hear you quit Lombardo and are going to make it rich in Hollywood."

"Herb Slaughter, how are you?"

"Hello Sally," he said as he leaned over and gave my mother a kiss on the lips. I could tell she did not receive his kiss as eagerly as she had received Sergeant's.

"This must be your son," he said.

"This is Herb, Walter. We got to know each other when I played out here six years ago after the Desert Inn just opened," my father said.

Herb sat down at the table. "I wish you luck in Hollywood. You're a brave man to make such a move. I wouldn't have the guts to do what you did." My father smiled as he accepted the compliment from his friend. "As for me, I like my steady job here at the Casino; they can't get rid of me; I owe them too much."

After Herb left, I asked my father what he meant.

"Herb's a permanent musician with the Desert Inn and plays for various shows. He's also an alcoholic and a gambler. His drinks and gambling debts are taken out of his salary and if he's lucky he'll get some money on payday."

My father wanted to leave for Los Angeles around four the next morning to get there in time to meet the moving van and arrange for our furniture to go into storage while we looked for a house. We went to bed early, got up before the sun, and left Vegas on a long straight road to LA. A few miles out of town, the sky was dark and the stars whose brilliance was blotted out by the neon lights of Vegas showed themselves again. I looked back on the city and wondered if it was trying to compete with the stars. My father was right—there is no place like Vegas. I laid my head on the back seat of the car to resume my interrupted sleep, and as I did the taste of the prime rib came back to me. I must have that again, I thought.

We got to LA around 11:00 AM and arranged for our furniture to go into storage. We stayed in a motel between Hollywood and North Hollywood. I forget the name. It was built into the mountain and in the back had little cabins that were larger than the rooms facing the highway. Directly across the freeway was the famous HOLLYWOOD sign. We took a cabin. While my parents went out looking for a house, I stayed at the motel to swim in the pool.

When I first went to the pool, there was a girl who I found out was a year older than I was. I forget her name but she was from East Lansing, Michigan, and was with her parents who had business in Hollywood. She was at the motel alone just as I was while her parents conducted their business. She was about my height, had shoulder length blonde hair, and a slender figure. I was immediately attracted to her. The fact that we were both alone at the motel heightened my blossoming sexuality, and I think her's, too. We frolicked in the pool together in that pre-mating dance that teenagers do when they are thrilled to be physically close to a person of the opposite sex but afraid to take it to the next step, or more honestly don't know how to. She was holding on to the rope that divided the deep end from the shallow end when I came up behind her and put my arms around her waist. She snuggled her head up against mine and my eyes look over her shoulder and saw her young, round breasts as her swimming suit bra pulled away from her chest. I lingered there enjoying the comfort and sight of her body. We spent about three days together, and then she left with her parents to go back to Michigan. We wrote to each other a few times but then lost contact.

One morning, I found a small gold metallic packet on the dresser in our cabin. It felt like there was a ring inside of it. I asked my father what it was and he told me in a reserved and somewhat embarrassed voice that it was a condom, what it was for, and how it was used. It was only time he ever talked to me about sex, and I was surprised mostly because I wasn't expecting it. I assumed that the last tenant of the cabin had left it there. It never entered my mind until later in my life that my parents were having sex as we crossed the country. We stayed in the same room but I never heard anything—then again, I'm a sound sleeper.

We found a house at 1328 North Gardner Street near Sunset Boulevard and only two miles from the Sunset Strip. The rent equaled our house payments in New York—one hundred and forty dollars a month. The house was the typical California bungalow with the living room, dining room, and kitchen on one side and the three bedrooms and bath on the other side separated by a hallway. It was a beige stucco house with dark brown trim. A garage separate from the house was in the back and the driveway was made of two strips of concrete with grass growing between the strips. In the back yard was an orange tree, but the oranges were inedible because there was not another orange tree of the opposite sex nearby to pollinate it. The house was a disappointment and come down for us. It was not as attractive or as big as our house in Roslyn. Yet, we were upbeat about our new life in this land of golden opportunity.

As the time drew nearer for Nana to rejoin us, I began to spend more time in my room thinking about the good time the three of us had coming across the country and re-tasting the prime rib. I began to regret that she would join us again. I noticed that my parents weren't talking to each other as much. Perhaps they were afraid to voice what we all knew. Maybe they were grieving, as I was, over losing this hallowed time we had enjoyed together. When we met Nana at the airport, I gave her a weak hug. As we walked toward the baggage claim area, I walked ahead of her in silence. "What's the matter, Walter, you don't look happy to see me," she said. I wasn't, but how could I tell her?

I concluded that while my grandmother was a wonderful force in my life and held our family together at times, she was also a major cause of our conflicts, and that maybe our lives would have been happier had Nana not lived with us. As I look back now, Nana was the *Jesus Nut* that kept us together, but she was also the *Jesus Nut* that failed, and in a manner of speaking caused us all to slip and fall.

Sally Smith, the author's mother at age 20

Sally Smith in her late 20s

Sadie Black, the author's grandmother at age 18

John Black, the author's grandfather

(From l to r) Guy Lombardo, the author, Walter C. Smith, the author's father on the author's tenth birthday, 1951, Roosevelt Grill, Hotel Roosevelt, New York City

Guy Lombardo with the author's father, Walter C. Smith circa 1955. Smith played trumpet and mellophone with Lombardo. The mellophone is similar to a French horn in shape, but produces a more mellow sound. Lombardo started doing TV shows in the early 1950s, and he did not like the fact that my father would have to stand with his side toward the audience in order for the microphones to be able to pick up the sound from curved bell of the mellophone. Lombardo, my father, and the Conn Music Company collaborated on how to rectify the problem. It was decided to pour hot lead in to the bell and straighten it out. However, this decision was not made without anxiety—it was feared that reshaping the horn would change its sound. Fortunately, it didn't, and pictured here is the first mellophone so designed. The design caught on and many high school bands started buying mellophones with a straighten bell.

My father playing the mellophone with Lombardo's Royal Canadians circa 1955.

The only picture I have of my father smiling.
He is on the far right. Date and situation is unknown.

Kenny Sargent (see chapter 4)

5

It's Not Easy Being Small

The Philistine came on and drew near to David, with his shield-bearer in front of him. When the Philistine looked and saw David, he disdained him, for he was only a youth, ruddy and handsome in appearance. The Philistine said to David, "Am I a dog, that you come to me with sticks?" And the Philistine cursed David by his gods.

I Sam 17:41–43

When the Philistine (Goliath) drew nearer to meet David, David ran quickly toward the battle line to meet the Philistine. David put his hand in his bag, took out a stone, slung it, and struck the Philistine on his forehead; the stone sank into his forehead, and he fell face down on the ground.

I Sam 17:48–49

I ALWAYS HAD A fondness for Kermit the Frog. His song about how difficult it was being green because you blend in with so many ordinary things, and people pass you over because they don't see you, could have been my song.[1] I would just have to exchange the word "green" with "small." It's not easy being small. You don't stand out, and people pass you over either because they don't see you or they don't take a small person seriously. Ralph Keyes in his book *The Height of Your Life*, quotes Harvard University professor, Mark Moore saying, "Large people's accomplishments are great works. Small people's accomplishments are the result of

---

1. *The Sesame Street Book and Record*. 'Green.' Lyrics by Joe Raposo, ©1970 Jonico Music, Inc.

a neurotic drive to succeed."[2] I often feel the need to prove that I am good at what I do, which is more difficult to do if the people I am trying to convince are taller than I am. Many people have said when I have given a powerful sermon, "My, that was a good sermon for a little guy," or if I express an opinion with a degree of passion they will say, "You're a feisty little fella, aren't you?" The emphasis is always on "little," and always comes from tall people. Keyes says, "Just as a tall person's body is public property, so is a short person's psyche." Sarcastic comments about a short person, even though no harm is intended, do more damage psychologically to the small person than those directed to the tall person.[3]

On the other hand, I found some advantages to my height. Clothing is easier for me to find than for some tall persons. I can sit comfortably in most cars, and the coach seats on a plane fit me perfectly. I notice that often people feel more comfortable in approaching me because of my height. Keyes says that tall people can have the problem of scaring others.[4] Yet, the best part of my height was when my sons were just beginning to walk. They could hold my hand without reaching high in the air as I noticed other children having to do with their tall dads. I can still feel my sons' hands wrapped around my index finger as we walked together. I thought if we could take these kinds of walks now, maybe in the future, if problems arose between us, we could trust each other to take walks that would be more difficult.

I also took solace in my grandmother's saying, "Big things come in small packages." I identified with David when he slew the giant Goliath. David was a small man; he was the smallest of his brothers but the Bible calls him, "A man after God's own heart."[5] As the years passed, I began to notice Jesus' emphasis on small things. The mustard seed is the smallest of all the seeds but grows into the largest of all trees.[6] Zaacheus was so small that he had to climb a tree to see Jesus. When Jesus passed by, he called Zaacheus down and goes to eat with him and in the process Zaacheus is transformed and becomes a giant of a man as he returns to people four

---

2. Keyes, Ralph. *The Height of Your Life*, Little Brown and Company, Boston-Toronto, 1980, 94.

3. Ibid., 74, 89.

4. Ibid., 77.

5. 1 Sam 13:13–14; 1 Sam 16:7.

6. Mark 4:31.

fold the money he had stolen from them.[7] Smallness was not a deterrent to Jesus. Jesus wasn't interested in your size; he cared more about whether or not you were faithful to God.

The struggle to accept my height (5'5.5"), however, was not easy. I didn't get to my present height until the end of high school, and along the way there were other factors that while not directly related to my height, nevertheless, contributed to a feeling of smallness and inadequacy.

In 1953, when I was twelve, I found myself standing with my pants and underpants pulled down to my ankles and my shirt up around my waist in front of my doctor and my mother. Dr. Bain, whose first name I never knew, was in his early fifties. He was about 5'7" tall, stocky but not fat, had dark brown hair around the sides of his head, and was bald on the top. He lived in a large white plantation-like house on a corner lot in Beacon Hill, the wealthy section at the time, of Port Washington, New York. He had built the house in the late 1940s, and when he did, it was the *talk-of-the-town*. "He must be making lots of money," I heard several people exclaim. I didn't know how he could make so much money when he only charged three dollars a visit, and often forgot to send a bill for those appointments that were not paid for at the time of the visit. When he built the house, he also built his office at the end of the house. The entrance to his office led to a rectangular waiting room whose walls were lined with dark maple wooden captain's chairs and the occasional table for holding the obligatory collection of outdated *Life* and *National Geographic* magazines that supposedly reduced your anxiety for having to be there. The room was bright with the help of five windows, two along the front wall and three on the sidewall. Every fifteen minutes or so, Dr. Bain would open the door leading to his examination room and say, "Who's next?"

As you walked into the examination room, Dr. Bain's desk was immediately in front of you in the left hand corner with a chair on the right side of the desk for the patient to sit. Next to the desk was a row of three windows, which were covered by semi-closed Venetian blinds that let enough light in to make the room bright and cheerful and still protect the privacy of undressed patients. In the middle of the room, was the examination table. Behind the table to the right was a three-panel white screen, the purpose of which I didn't know at that time. There was a counter and white metal glassed cabinets along the back wall with medical supplies.

---

7. Luke 19:1–10.

I entered the room with my mother. Dr. Bain took his seat behind his desk and my mother took the chair beside the desk and pulled it out so that she was directly facing the doctor. I was told to stand in between them, drop my pants, and raise my shirt. This forced nudity in front of my mother and the doctor was embarrassing. They leaned over and looked directly at my genitals. The doctor took my small scrotum into his hand and with his fingers gently felt the sack.

"Sally," he said to my mother, "they're not developing. Here, feel for yourself."

Oh, my God, he's going to let my mother examine me, I thought, as I felt a wave of panic reverberate throughout my body. I was afraid of what would happen if she touched me. Please don't touch me, Mom, I pleaded inwardly.

I looked down as her hand came closer to my tiny scrotum. Her bright blue eyes peered intently at my genitals. The V-neck of her white silk blouse revealed the cleavage of her full breasts and the straps of her bra that were supporting them. Her beauty made me realize how much I loved her. My fear melted away in the heat of my love, and I now wanted her to touch all of me. I wanted to fall into her arms, kiss her, tell her I loved her, and that I would never treat her as her husband did, that I would take care of her all the days of her life. Her hand touched my scrotum lightly and was soon withdrawn.

"You're right, Dr. Bain. What can we do?" she said, interrupting my fantasies and reminding me there was another man in the room.

"Sally, I would like to give Walter a series of hormone injections over the next several months to see if we can get his testicles to develop."

The injections, given in my arm, started that day and continued every two weeks for the next three months. On every visit, there was the genital examination by the doctor and my mother, except my mother just looked, and didn't touch me. Finally, my testicles descended, making my mother ecstatic.

"You're well on your way to becoming a man," she said as we drove home.

Becoming a man was the furthest thing from my mind. What I took from this experience besides the humiliation, was a ton of anxiety over not knowing what was going on, and the confirmation that something was wrong with me. At least, the shots helped me to grow an inch. Being a pint sized version of my age, another inch gave me hope that I would not end up as a midget. At this point, I'd be willing to stand naked in front of the whole world if it could add more inches to my height. I was the smallest in my class, even among the girls, and the appearance of my testicles, were the least of my worries.

As I look back on this event now, I wonder what made it so traumatic? My mother did nothing that any concerned mother would not have done under the same circumstances. I know as parents, my wife and I looked for signs that our sons were developing normally including their sexuality, not in a voyeuristic sense, but as concerned parents who need to know what is happening with their children. We also kept an eye out for drug use, monitored whom they chose as friends, and what they watched on television. And what twelve year-old boy wouldn't be embarrassed to be nude in front of his mother and doctor as they examined the most intimate part of his body?

It wasn't only the nudity, however, that scared me. What frightened me were my overwhelming feelings of love for my mother. They came out of nowhere, ambushing me. I had never had such powerful feelings before. Years later, in college, I would learn that Sigmund Freud said it was normal for boys to want to make love to their mothers. At the age of twelve, however, I didn't know you could think such things, and I didn't know how to control them. Besides, how could I take my mother to bed to make love to her when I knew nothing about sexual intercourse and my genitals were undeveloped? What made it worse was that these feelings were being experienced in front of an audience—the doctor, who I was convinced, knew what I was thinking. Not only did he see me naked but he was also witnessing the blooming of my sexuality before I even had time to understand what was happening. What should have been the most private of moments was on public display.

I was also at the stage where I was not able to separate my feelings from my mother's feelings. I couldn't imagine that we had separate feelings. I naturally concluded that my feelings for her were the same feelings she had for me. It never crossed my mind that she might not have had any sexual desire for me as she examined my genitals with the doctor. If my mother's feelings and mine were the same and I couldn't control my feelings, surely I couldn't control my mother's. That combined that with the lack of sexual development, made me feel powerless in front of the woman I loved the most.

That powerlessness translated in later years into my desire to have sexual relations with the few girls I dated—a need to show my potency. But no matter how intimate we became, I could never bring myself to become sexually one with any girl. The passion of the moment urged going all the way, but then, for some unknown reason, a picture of a baby entered my mind. I didn't want to be a father at my young age, I decided. In hindsight, that was good, because I escaped unwanted fatherhood, and the girl escaped unwanted motherhood. However, I also wondered if that image of a baby also reflected my feelings of inadequacy not only in being a father but also in being a man and a husband.

I was also scared because I didn't know what was going on. No one told me what my testicles were for or why they needed developing. Was there something wrong with me that I couldn't be trusted with that information? From what were they protecting me? How reassuring it would have been if they had simply told me about sexual intercourse, and that I was at the stage where I was developing a man's body so that one day I would join my life with a woman and through our love produce children. Moreover, what was happening to me happens from time-to-time, but don't worry because we can do something about it. Instead, the lack of knowledge when combined with the sexual intimacy of the situation, whether real or imagined, produced a powerful feeling that said I was inadequate before men and women, and in order to be cured I had to suffer humiliation.

Years later, this experience came to symbolize the importance of telling the truth. The Apostle Paul says in his letter to the Ephesians that we should speak the truth in love to each other so that we can grow more in every way and be like Christ.[8] Jesus also says, "If you continue as my disciples, you will know the truth and the truth will set you free."[9] Knowing the truth in my situation would have set me free from my anxieties of inadequacy instead of leading me to doubt my own worth. It would have saved me from years of anger toward my mother, and from being suspicious of others', especially women's, intentions toward me. If I couldn't trust my mother, who could I trust? Instead of taking sixty years to forgive her, I might have been able to do it sooner, be reconciled to her, and enjoyed her for the mother God meant her to be.

---

8. Eph 4:1–5.
9. John 8:32.

I was not only small for my age, but I was also the youngest in my class. I entered Kindergarten at Public School 32 (PS32) in Flushing, New York in 1945 at the age of four years and ten months. The other kids in my class ranged from two months to over a year older than I was. We then moved to Glen Cove, Long Island in the summer of 1946, where I was enrolled in first grade at the Glen Cove Elementary School.

Miss McGow was my first grade teacher. She was sixty-four, a small framed woman with grey hair and wire rim glasses. She never married, retired the next year, and died the year after.

I was sitting in the next to the last desk of the second row from the inside wall of the classroom. It was our first day at school, and Miss McGow told us to write down what she wrote on the blackboard. Not knowing what she meant, I scribbled on my paper and handed it in to her. At the end of the day, she gave me a note to take home to my mother. I don't recall what transpired next, but I do remember my mother complaining about the principal to my grandmother.

"That stupid ass wants to put Walter back into kindergarten because he can't write his name and he's too young for first grade. I told him to go to hell. My son was going to stay in first grade."

And, in first grade I stayed, but the deal was that my mother would teach me to read and write, which she faithfully did for several months. I didn't like the idea of having to work another hour after school to catch up with the other kids, but being with my mother made it worthwhile. It was the first time I remember we spent significant time together. There were kisses, hugs, "I love yous," and snacks when I did well. I became a good speller. All through elementary school, I got nothing less than an "A" on spelling tests. However, no matter how hard she tried or I tried, I never caught up. For the next three years, a teacher came into my classroom and called my name, and I would leave for remedial work. The other kids got to stay, and they knew why I was leaving. Having to leave made me feel that I wasn't as good as the other kids. I didn't realize at the time that what was wrong was my young age. If I had been six months older, I could have managed the work. I started school being behind and I never caught up until my post-graduate years. It's like the football team that trails 28-0 at half time. They can still win the game, but they have to make four touchdowns just to tie the game and hope the other team doesn't score anymore. That's a huge task, and that's what school felt like for me.

I barely made it through high school, and I got into college through the community college system. I graduated with C's. I was accepted at San Francisco Theological Seminary not based on my grades, but by the fact that my church deemed me fit to be a minister. I graduated from seminary with a C plus average, and I got my Doctor of Ministry degree at the age of forty-one with an A- average. I began to see that my academic troubles were not due to my lack of intelligence, but to the fact that I was too young to understand what I was asked to understand. In one respect, that was reassuring. In another respect, my insight came too late. When my colleagues gave me a party to celebrate my receiving the Doctor of Ministry degree and respected my accomplishment, I could only see it as a consolation prize. My grades were never good enough to get me into a Ph.D. program, which I would have liked. In my mind, I took second best. I thought of all the subjects that interested me that I never tried because I couldn't begin to understand them. Or the things I could have accomplished, the worlds I could have explored, if only I had started school a year later. Maybe God wanted me to be a pastor and there is nothing wrong with that. In this day, however, when pastors are ranked lower in trust than used-car salesmen and paid a lot less, I sometimes wonder just what I've accomplished.

I discovered recently that I have a condition called X-linked Hypophosataemic Rickets. Simply put, it means the kidneys fail to absorb phosphorous from food. Phosphorous is a key chemical that promotes bone growth and the healing of broken bones. The X-link means that it is a genetically inherited condition from my mother's X chromosome. People with this condition are often small in stature, and have numerous abscesses and cavities in their teeth. Often an abscess in a tooth can occur spontaneously. My mother had lost all of her teeth by the time she was twenty, and I had lost most of mine by the time I was twenty-nine.

I was also born with rickets. My legs were bowed so severely that the doctors recommended breaking my legs and resetting them. My mother would have nothing to do with it because of the pain it would cause me and the fact that I would be in a body cast for six months. The doctors then suggested that she take me to the beach and walk me on the rocks and let me sit in the sun. My mother told me how I cried when she forced me to walk on the rough rocks at the beach. "It broke my heart to see you in pain," she said. I couldn't understand why she didn't want to put me through the pain of having my legs broken when I would be under anesthetic, but was willing to walk me on the rocks and listen to my screams. I don't how it happened but my legs straightened out.

People with X-linked Hypophosataemic Rickets are athletically challenged. While my legs straightened out, they never developed strength. I jokingly tell people (my victims—usually jocks), with a straight face, that in high school I held the record for the hundred yard dash—fifteen seconds flat. I enjoy watching their reaction. Anyone who knows track and field will realize that rate is about five seconds over a slow runner. Many of the kids were resting at the finish line while I was just crossing the fifty-yard line. My victims at this point are put in an awkward position. They don't know if they should congratulate me or tell me they know that I was a slow runner. I also couldn't jump, climb ropes, or do pull-ups. When I was in seminary during the Viet Nam War, some of my classmates felt guilty for having a ministerial deferment from the draft. I never felt guilty for mine. I knew that I would never make it in the armed services. If I passed the physical, I wouldn't make it past the first day of boot camp. In my way of thinking, my ministerial deferment saved my country a lot of money from having to process a weakling only to have to discard him. I was doing my part to help my country even as I marched in several protest parades. As I write this section, I'm in a motel room at Virginia Beach. The sun is shining and I hear the ocean waves just outside my door, which I have opened. Overhead, I hear the roar of fighter jets taking off from the nearby Oceana Naval Air Station. Every time the jets go over, I think of how strong the pilots have to be to fly one of those machines. I envy them their strength.

I questioned the justice of all this. The older I became, the more I resented my mother fighting for me to start school before I was ready. Even if I started later, that wouldn't have helped my physical stature and the problems associated with it, but I might have been able to do better academically, and, at least, have one part of my life I could feel good about. As a result, I was a loser both academically and athletically. During my growing up, people, including my mother, told me I was a wonderful boy. I wondered what they saw in me. They didn't know the real me, and they didn't take the time to find out. I learned quickly that being a good boy was what I was expected to be. But I also blamed God. Why, God, did you give me such a lousy body when I'm a good kid? You know that I love you and I go to Sunday School. My teachers think I'm wonderful, but you don't seem to think so. What kind of a God are you who does such lousy bodywork? As I write this, I'm sixty-three and more confident in my abilities, at least the mental and interpersonal parts, but I resent the fact that most of my life was such an uphill struggle, one that didn't have to happen.

∼

The summer after my testicles descended, I discovered masturbation. I had never heard the word and would not for another five years in spite of receiving sex education in the ninth grade. It was a hot, humid summer day as I climbed into the bathtub in the afternoon. I reasoned if I was going to be wet from perspiration, it would be better in the bathtub where I could cool off and play with my toy boats. My penis erected and I wondered what it would feel like if I put soap on it and rubbed it. My hand first rubbed the head of my penis, which caused all kinds of tingling sensations and spasms in my body that I had never experienced before, but found enjoyable until a milky white substance shot out. I thought I had broken something and it scared me. I didn't dare tell my parents or my grandmother. What would they think about me? I was bad, rotten, and filthy as I heard my mother describe me at other times. I best keep this a secret, and hope that I don't die from my insides oozing out of my penis. I bet my father never did anything like this, I thought. I'll never do this again, I told myself as I quickly washed off the expelled substance so that my mother or grandmother would not see it if they came into the bathroom. But the next day, I couldn't resist. Neither could I resist in the days following. While this act scared me because I didn't know what it was, it was also liberating. I was finding something enjoyable in life, and it was my own body.

As I look back now, this may have been God's way of preparing me to accept myself, to enjoy the life God had given me, and to enjoy God. Years later, as part of my healing, my counselor, a Baptist pastoral counselor, had me focus on those things that brought me pleasure and a sense of accomplishment. He taught me to take delight in myself and find happiness with the person God created in God's own image. I was also proud of the day I told my sons about masturbation and how it was normal and nothing to fear. I saved them from some of the anxieties I experienced, and I helped them to see that masturbation was one of God's many ways of making them the men God wanted them to be.

Not long after my new experience, my mother had four women friends over for dessert. It was a warm, summer day. With no air conditioning, I was dressed in shorts and a skimpy shirt. The long living room of our house was in the back of the house facing west so the afternoon sun shown through the large picture window, facing our next-door neighbor. My mother called me to introduce me to her friends. The high blue armchair sat at the corner of the picture window allowing anyone looking our way to have an unobstructed view into our living room. My mother put her arm around my waist and drew me to her breast. "This is my son, little Walter . . . I wouldn't know what to do without him." She was treating me like a baby not as person entering puberty. She put her hand up my shorts and adjusted one side of my underwear. Sliding her hand across my genitals, she adjusted the other side. I didn't mind these forays into my private region when I was a child, but now I froze in fear. Only afterwards could I put words to my feelings. My god, I'm helpless, I thought. She might pull my pants down in front of these women. The women tried not to look. They reminded me of nurses who look at the ceiling or above your head when you are exposed, trying not to embarrass you. However, by not looking they reinforce the fact that you are undressed and vulnerable. I noticed these women, while trying not to look, couldn't help taking a glance at me. Did they want to see my penis? I thought. What will happen if they do? Would they know that I'd been masturbating? I pulled myself away from my mother, as politely as I could (remember, I'm a good boy), and went upstairs to my room where I sat in my chair shaking.

For years, I wondered why my mother had to adjust my underwear in front of other women. Did she want to show her women friends my newly descended testicles, which she had worked so hard to get? She was proud of the fact that I was on my way to becoming a man, but then she also treated me like a baby, holding me close, calling me 'little Walter,' and violating my private space. Who was I—a man or a little boy? It made me wonder if all those sexual feelings I had for her as she examined me with the doctor were just my feelings, or was I also right in thinking that she was enjoying the experience and wanted me as a secret lover. Why couldn't I be like other kids who can play ball with their friends? I was scared that I wasn't normal.

Having a child's mind, I considered much of what was happening to me was because there was something wrong with me. Such things wouldn't happen if I were a better son, and if I were, maybe God would have given me a better mother. Was God disappointed in me, too? Maybe God was as disappointed in me as he was in the world he created when he brought the Flood to destroy the earth. I began to wonder if I should not be destroyed, too. What good was I to God or anybody else? Maybe my mother was sent by God to destroy me. If she was, she was doing a good job.

The trouble with children's minds is that their egocentricity causes them to think they are the cause of everything that happens to them. When my sons were a year old, I held them in my arms so they could turn the light switch on and off. They were ecstatic; they thought they had the power to control the lights, and I'm sure they thought they controlled the world. They had no idea that it took millions of miles of wire and the labor of thousands to make the lights work. When we are abused as children, we assume it is not the abusive adult who has problems, but that we did something to deserve it. Over the course of my ministry, I've been amazed at the number of people who described to me how a parent or a relative beat them when they were a child. When I suggested the beating was abusive, most replied, "But I deserved it." To which I replied, "No one deserves that kind of punishment." As we grow into adulthood, we take those childhood ideas with us. We grow physically, have the appearance of adults, and are able to produce children, but those early childhood images and ideas don't mature with us. Our unworthiness as children becomes our unworthiness as adults. So we continue to believe that we are the cause of our problems. Even in adult years when something bad happens to us we will assume, at first, that it is our fault. It took me years to realize that my mother's abuse and humiliation of me was not my fault.

But how do you rid yourself of this egocentricity? Regardless of what anyone says, when you hurt, it's hard to think of something beyond yourself; it's hard to see another's point of view. You just want to get even. When I was in my mid-forties, I came to the full realization of the negative effects my mother's abuse had on me. Nothing would have given me more satisfaction than to see her suffer as much as she made me suffer. But she never did. She lived out her life without knowing, in spite of my attempts to tell her of the hell she put me through every day. I called her several times to talk to her about her abuse of me. What appears below is a typical conversation.

"Hi, Mom."

"Oh, hi, Walt, how are you doing?"

"Not too well."

"What's the matter?"

"I've been going through hell, Mom. Do you realize what you did to me as a kid? You were always adjusting my underwear in front of other women? You scared the shit out of me, Mom. I was afraid you would pull my pants down in front of them."

"Oh, that's a bunch of bullshit. You make up the most fantastic stories. You just want to hurt me."

"No, I don't. It is you who have hurt me, like the time you told me I was no longer your son if I had anything to do with my father."

"I never said that to you. Why do you lie? You've always been a liar—you're just like your rotten father."

"I'm not a liar. You never call, you forget your grandchildren's birthdays, and you didn't even tell me that you and Dick (her brother) were coming to visit Anna and we lived only 500 miles away—we could have come to see you, but you didn't let us know that you would be so close. My kids don't know you. What do you expect me to think?"

"Go to hell." And with that she hung up.

It's like the book of Ecclesiastes that says that the evil person gets along just as well as a good person.[10] So what's the point of doing anything? Why not just take a gun and shoot the bitch? But, I'm her son and a pastor. The Ten Commandments tell me to honor my father and mother, but how can you honor them if they don't honor you? I'm drawn to the Apostle Paul who in Ephesians admonishes children to honor their father and mother but then goes on to say: "Fathers (and I assume this would include mothers), do not provoke your children to anger, but bring them up in the discipline and instruction of the Lord."[11] It's a two way street—to be honored, one must honor. As a pastor, I'm also under the obligation to forgive. How could I possibly be a pastor and preach about forgiveness, one of the central aspects of the Christian faith, when I couldn't do it myself? I wondered if this faith that I had committed myself to had anything to offer me in doing this impossible task.

---

10. Eccl 9.
11. Eph 6:1–4.

One of the events that enabled me to deal with my own egocentricity was the death in 1992, of my former boss, Clem Lamberth, a day before his sixtieth birthday. Clem was nine years older than I was, and he was an extraordinary churchman who held his staff is high regard and trusted them to do their work and we didn't disappoint him. When he died, I not only lost a friend, but the Presbyterian Church (U.S.A.) also lost one of its greatest leaders. At his funeral, his friend, Jack Robinson, a retired Presbyterian pastor, preached the sermon. He spoke of what we were all thinking; why did Clem have to die so young when he had so much more to give? Then Robinson said something I will never forget. He said, "I'm sure that when we meet God face-to-face, God will answer all our questions, if, after seeing God in all his glory, we still have them."

Could it be, I thought, that there might be a greater reality than my experience of the abuse from my mother? Would I come to a time when, while I would never forget what happened, it would no longer control my life? Would I be able to allow the vastness and the beauty of life to supplant my pain and suffering? Is this what God was saying to Job, a righteous man who suffered the loss of family, fortune, and physical health for no reason at all when God overwhelmed Job with his majesty and might?

"Where were you when I laid the foundations of the earth?" God says, expecting an answer from Job. "Tell me if you have understanding. Who determined its measurements, surely you know! Who stretched the line upon it . . . who laid the cornerstone?"[12]

Couldn't God at least commiserate with Job, put his arm around him, comfort him, and tell him why he was suffering? The truth of the matter is that God doesn't have the answer for why Job suffered because there is NO answer. However, God shows Job the enormity of what God created, and in the process shows Job that he is part of this expansive and beautiful universe created by a God who is so big and so full of majesty that there is no other like him. God moves Job to a higher level of understanding where Job's sufferings, while important, are far less important than God.

I knew if I was going to deal with my mother's abuse, I had to come to grips with the fact that I may not be the most important thing in the world. I may be the apple of God's eye, but I'm not the only apple. My egocentricity led me to believe that I was abused because I was bad and deserved it. What would happen if I stopped thinking that I was the center

12. Job 38:4–6.

of the universe; that I controlled everything? Would I stop blaming myself and start seeing that maybe I was abused because my mother had her own inner conflicts and pain, and I just happened to be on the receiving end of how she was working out her own problems? That's not to excuse what she did, but once I got out of the way and stopped blaming myself, I started on the road to forgiving her.

6

No Place to Hide: The Call to the Ministry

Now the word of the LORD came to me saying, "Before I formed you in the womb I knew you, and before you were born I consecrated you; I appointed you a prophet to the nations." Then I said, "Ah, Lord GOD! Truly I do not know how to speak, for I am only a boy." But the LORD said to me, "Do not say, 'I am only a boy'; for you shall go to all to whom I send you, and you shall speak whatever I command you. Do not be afraid of them, for I am with you to deliver you, says the LORD."

JER 1:4–8

"JOE, HOW MUCH CHEMISTRY do you need to be a doctor?" I asked as we walked together up the steep, tree-lined hill to report to work at the Hollywood Bowl. It was the summer of 1960. Joe was the head usher on the second promenade, and I was an usher on the first. I made $2.50 a night, which wasn't good money for two hours of work even in 1960. However, the opportunity to hear the Rudolph Serkins, Jasha Heifeitzs, Oscar Levants, and many other greats in the musical world along with the opportunity to greet Will and Auriel Durant, Pat Brown, the Governor of California, Robert Young, Walt Disney, Norma Shearer, and others made that paltry sum seem to be a thousand times greater. Joe was 5'10" tall, stocky, black hair, and of Italian descent. He had just completed his second year as a medical student at the University of Southern California, and I had just completed my first year of college as a pre-med major in which I failed chemistry.

"You eat, sleep, and drink it, Walter."

"Thanks," I said, as I continued walking. Inwardly, I was stumbling, gasping, trying to catch the breath Joe's words, now swirling around me, sucked out of my lungs. It reminded me of the time, ten years earlier, when a kid held my head under water. My arms and legs cut violently through the salt water trying to get out of his grasp. Time stopped. In my pure reactive state, my only thought was to survive. Joe's words came quickly, and I felt myself drowning again. Their meaning was unambiguous and left no room for me to ask, but Joe, couldn't I just get by with a few classes? My liking for Joe turned to loathing. He was smart, tall, and handsome, and even though we shared the handsome part, I felt short and dumb. He was already in medical school and he was blocking me from going. I wanted to tear him from limb to limb so he could feel the pain that I was feeling. All my life I had wanted to be a doctor. I had never thought of any other profession. The idea that I would have to take so much chemistry, coupled with the realization that I wasn't good at it, made me feel that my high school guidance counselor was right when she told me two years earlier, after looking at my grades, "You're a loser, Walter. You'll never amount to anything—don't even try to go to college, you'll never graduate." I had a lot of F's on my transcript. They came from Roslyn High School in Roslyn, New York. I had passed all my classes there with C's and B's, but at the end of each school year, we had to take the Regent's exams. Whatever you made on that exam, was your grade for the year. I was never good at taking tests—they made me nervous, and the Regent's exams made me more nervous when I thought that a whole year's worth of studying could vanish with a poor showing on one test. In my anxiety, I doubted my answers, often changing a correct answer to a wrong one. I tried to explain that to my counselor and even showed her my actual grades. I remember sitting in a chair by the side of her desk, but it felt like I was standing naked on a box while she walked around me yelling at me that I was no good. Maybe she was trying to motivate this quiet, unassuming high school student, but I felt like I was being whipped. I wanted to cry. I wanted to scream, You don't know me, you bitch. You don't give a damn about me, and you're too ignorant to take the time to find out.

Part of me shriveled up, trembling in the face of the reality that I might be worthless. But part of me, also, found strength to fight back. Somehow, I knew she was wrong. I imagined myself graduating Magna Cum Laude from medical school, throwing my diploma in her face, telling her she was a lousy counselor, and should be driven out of the school system. But, of course, that was at least ten years into the future and no good to me in the present. So I did what I could—I didn't give her the satisfaction of a response. I didn't blink an eye or shed a tear. I just quietly walked out of her office knowing that I would not only go to college but graduate. As I think about my response to Joe, it wasn't Joe or his answer that I hated—what I hated was the fact that my failing chemistry might be a confirmation of my counselor's prophesy.

"Stand up straight, and keep those shirts tucked in," Alvin, our head usher barked his usual command before we took our stations, jarring me from my preoccupation with Joe's answer. The shirts he referred to were our uniform shirts. They were tan and came in one size—large. I was 5'5" and 110 pounds and the shirt was almost as big as I was. The shirttail was so long that I couldn't tuck it all down my trouser legs. Part of it crumpled up below my waist making me look like I had a grotesque growth on my lower abdomen. Rubber bands wrapped around my upper arms kept the sleeve length at least manageable.

Alvin was a tall man with balding black hair who looked about forty even though he was only in his mid-twenties. He never smiled, and when he said something it was usually in the form of a criticism. The ushers used to joke that we didn't think he would know a feeling if he ran into one. Tonight things were going well and he didn't have anything to complain about, but it didn't stop him from giving us his usual final instruction, as if we didn't know better. I walked through the vine-covered arch to get to my station, which was at the other end of the semi-curved promenade. The sun shone directly into my eyes so I moved quickly to where one of the giant speaker towers was casting a shadow and slowed my gait. I couldn't get Joe's answer out of my head. I tried telling myself that he was only kidding.

"Good evening, Doctors Durant. May I help you with anything this evening?" Will and Auriel Durant were historians and philosophers who co-authored many books including *The Story of Civilization*, an eleven volume set on the history of the world. I was always happy to see the Durants. At this stage in their life, they were a cute, old couple.

"No thank you, son," this white haired and mustached man replied. He and Auriel took their seats in the box next to where I was stationed. They said little to each other as they opened their picnic basket and took out their supper. They ate slowly and occasionally sipped on a glass of wine. I had read an article about the Durants in a local magazine before the summer began. I couldn't believe that I was in the presence of such greatness. I marveled at their grasp of history, but I think I marveled more at their quietness. They hardly said a word to each other, and I never heard a discussion of history flowing from their box. Maybe they had said it all in the volumes they had written and there was nothing more to say. A few years later, when I was in seminary, a friend of mine gave me Volume VI of *The Story of Civilization—The Reformation*. How I wish I had it when I was at the Hollywood Bowl so I could have had them autograph it. When they died, I thanked God for their lives, and for the opportunity just to be in their presence. Their quiet and assuming manner stood in stark contrast to the demeaning assault of my high school counselor. Without knowing it, they silently offered me a glimpse of my potential that I was determined to achieve.

I left at intermission. It was a long walk to Hollywood and Highland where I could catch a bus home, but at the age of nineteen, it didn't bother me. Unaware of what the Durants symbolized for me, and without any prospects on the horizon for another career, I felt my life coming to an end. I worried about what my family would think if I didn't become a doctor. My father had wanted to be one, too, before he decided on a career in music mostly because he didn't have the grades and he needed the money to support his new wife. My God, am I part of a family of losers? I thought. My mother and grandmother couldn't think of a better profession for me. I would make lots of money and have prestige in the community, and they would have the thrill of saying, "Oh, that's my son (grandson), the doctor." But I also wanted to be a doctor—medical matters fascinated me. When my doctor looked into my ears, I wanted to see what he was seeing. Even today, when I have had to have minor surgical procedures, I'll ask the surgeon if I can watch. He usually says, "Sure," just before putting me to sleep.

In elementary school, I thought I would be a general practitioner. That's all the doctors were in those days except for the few who specialized in surgery or psychiatry, but I didn't know anything about the latter. As I grew older, I thought I would like to be a baby doctor—that is, the one who delivers babies. I had no idea of the obstetrics/gynecology specialty, and how babies got out of their mothers' bodies was still a mystery to me even at fourteen. Then I heard of a specialty called pathology. These were the doctors who did autopsies and figured out why people died. The idea of solving a mystery intrigued me as did being able to see what a body looked like on the inside. I always had a curiosity about what things look like on the inside. I enjoyed, and still do, removing the covers of radios, computers, and other instruments to see how they're put together.

I first took chemistry in high school. Our teacher, Miss Evelyn Christie, was thirty years old and working on a Ph.D. in Chemistry at the University of California at Los Angeles (UCLA), or as we humorously called it, the United Cookie and Loaf Association. We heard that she was brilliant, and wanted a career in research chemistry. She was teaching to pay her college bills. She walked with a definite gait, but halted every so often as if she was hesitating. On the one hand, she gave the impression that she was sure of herself, but on the other that she wasn't. She was 5'4" tall, had blond hair, blue eyes, and always wore high heels, a white blouse that accentuated her large breasts, and a straight skirt, usually red, brown, or gray, that accentuated her curvaceous hips, and activated the hormones of the teenage boys who were in her presence. She managed to kill questions in the class by assigning the student who asked the question the project of coming up with the answer and writing a two hundred-fifty word paper on the subject. Except for the one or two brilliant students in the class who loved to write reports, and, therefore, didn't hesitate to ask questions, we kept our mouths shut. I forget what grade I got in the class, but whatever the grade was, it didn't discourage me from medicine.

I entered Los Angeles City College in the fall of 1959, and proudly put on my application that I was a pre-med major. I felt important—I was going to be somebody, and prove to that old bitch of a guidance counselor that she was wrong about me. The first day of the semester, I walked into the lecture hall for my chemistry class. I was overwhelmed because I had never seen classrooms so big. Soon, ninety-nine other students joined me as we waited quietly, since no one knew each other, for the professor to arrive. I think his last name was Stevenson. He was a tall, thin man with black hair who resembled Abraham Lincoln. He was about fifty-five years old and had the personality of a cornered gorilla. He announced that in his class there was no room for error. "If you're going to work in chemistry, you have to be perfect, precise, and careful," he thundered. "One little mistake could kill you or severely injure you. I know this, because a friend of mine was blinded in a chemistry lab because he made a stupid mistake." To emphasize his concern, for our own safety, he said that all problems (mathematical) handed in for homework or completed on a test had to be perfect. One error and the whole problem would be counted wrong. He didn't believe in giving partial credit, which meant that if a student added

4.3 grams to 5.6 grams and came out with the correct answer of 9.9 grams but had written down 43 grams and forgot the decimal point, the whole problem was counted wrong. From that day on, I began to fail chemistry. Three weeks before the semester ended, I asked him what grade I would get if I dropped the class. He said, "An 'F.'" I figured I wouldn't do much better in the remaining three weeks, and there was no sense in putting myself through the agony of studying for the final exam, so I dropped the class, which put me on academic probation. I wasn't alone. Out of the one hundred students in the class, ninety-seven received F's; one received a D, one a C, and one a B. I retook the class with a professor who was short and fat. I passed with a C.

Several years later, in my first semester in seminary, a few of my classmates and I were sitting on the second floor deck outside of the dining room looking into a sea of green trees with some of the seminary buildings poking their roofs out from behind the branches. It was a warm, sunny fall day and we were talking about how we decided to go into the ministry. I shared my chemistry story. One of my classmates was Japanese, by the name of Takarabe. We called him "Tak."

"You had old, grumpy Stevenson in chemistry, too? So did I and I got an 'F.' I went on to UCLA and majored in chemistry and graduated Magna Cum Laude. One of my professors told me that Stevenson should be fired because he discouraged so many good students from going into chemistry. You shoulda stuck with it, Walter, and not let that jerk discourage you."

A wave of regret swept over me. I'm a loser I thought, just like my counselor said I was. I don't have what it takes. I could be in medical school now if I hadn't let that soulless professor discourage me. What kind of a professor fails ninety-seven percent of his class? How could he live with himself? How can I live with myself? But then I remembered I didn't particularly like chemistry. I thought it was a fascinating subject, but it didn't capture my passion. It was like when I stopped taking piano lessons after ten years of study. My last teacher was a concert pianist, and I was one of her two best students. I concluded that I would have to practice not one but six to eight hours a day if I was to make a career as a pianist. I couldn't see myself doing that partly because I knew how hard it was to get into the music business from the experiences of my father, partly because of the political wars of the concert arena my teacher told me about, but also because I didn't have the passion for it. I didn't wake up in the morning wanting to get to the piano. If I continued, I knew I would be good, but I would only be technically good. What did capture my passion was the church.

∼

When we moved into our house on North Gardner Street in Hollywood in August of 1957, my mother said, "There's a pretty pink church up on the corner a few blocks over. Let's all go to church this Sunday, maybe God will bring us good luck." Even at my young age of fifteen, I had the feeling that this was not the way God worked. While God would be pleased to see us in church, God would not lavish on us great rewards. That Sunday my mother, father, and I went to church. The pink church was an old, almost gothic-like building on the corner of Sunset and Martel. We had to climb eight cement steps to get to the main entrance. As we started up the steps a huge hand, which seemed to come out of the heavens, reached down and pulled us in. As we looked up, we saw a tall, broad man with white hair smiling at us.

"Welcome to the West Hollywood Presbyterian Church," he said. "My name is Ralph White (I'm not sure of his last name) and who might you be?" We told him our names. "I'm so glad you're here. "Oh Morrie, come here. This is Morrie Dragna, his son Mark should be around here someplace."

"I'm afraid he didn't make it to church this morning, Ralph. You know how these teenagers are, but obviously this teenager is different."

Morrie was a tall man with a dark complexion and a thick head of black hair that was combed up and straight back. His wife, Kathryn, was confined to bed with a heart condition. Morrie sold supplies to grocery stores and a year later would be instrumental in my getting a job at Ralph's Grocery store and would be one of the Elders to ordain me nine years in the future. "I'm so glad to meet you folks. Oh, there's Bill Cleghorn, they just moved into town a few months ago. Bill, come over and meet some new folks."

Bill introduced us to his wife and four children, who were between the ages of ten and sixteen. As we were talking, a man in a black, pin stripe suit, white shirt, and thin black tie walked up and introduced himself as Ross Greek, the pastor of the church. Ross was a few inches taller than me, had salt and pepper hair, and was almost as round as he was tall. He smiled broadly, and I noticed that the tooth just behind his eyetooth on his right upper jaw was missing. When he found out my name was Walter, he said jokingly, "Oh, you must be a pole vaulter," and gave out a laugh that came directly from his belly that made you think you were in the presence of Santa Claus. He told me, after I got to know him, that he never had a bridge made for that lost tooth, not because he didn't have the money, but because, "God needed my money more than I needed a tooth."

The next Tuesday afternoon, Greek visited us in our new home. I had been in the backyard shooting my BB rifle, and when I came in the house, I saw this strange man in a black, pin stripe suit, white shirt and thin black tie sitting in my grandmother's favorite chair. It took me awhile to remember who he was. He jumped up, to shake my hand. After we sat back down, he wanted to know what I liked, what I wanted to study, what grade I was in, and how I liked California.

He told us that he was raised a Quaker in Ohio and attended Ohio State University where he played football, although he was not too good at it. After Ohio State, he taught at the Finley School for Boys and then decided to go into the ministry. After graduating from Seminary, he went into the Navy as a Chaplain and served during WWII. He decided to become a Presbyterian because the Quakers did not have a professional ordained ministry. He liked the Presbyterian Church because of the emphasis on education, mission, Biblical scholarship, and the just way in which they govern the church, which is evidenced by the fact that the Constitution of the United States is modeled after that of the Presbyterian Church. His family consisted of his wife, Norma, and his two children Ross, 11, and Dana, 6. He then said that he hoped we would join the church. "It's a small congregation, but the people love each other." He didn't think we could find a better church anywhere else, and he would write for our letter of transfer from the Congregational Church we were attending in Manhasset, New York. My mother took a liking to Ross, and she assured him that we would join the church and the next Sunday we did. The following week Ross was back at our front door with some books in his hands.

"Walter, we need a Sunday school teacher for the fifth grade. I think you'd be a good one. How about teaching for us?"

"But, Reverend Greek, I don't know how to teach. I'm only fifteen years old."

"God will teach you how to teach. Sunday school starts a week from Sunday. See you there."

He handed me the books and left. When the prophet Jeremiah was told by God that God had appointed him to be a prophet to the nations,

Jeremiah protested by saying, "Ah, Lord God! Truly, I do not know how to speak, for I am only a boy." (It is assumed that Jeremiah was only sixteen when he was called by God.) God thundered back, "Do not say, 'I am only a boy'; for you shall go to all to whom I send you, and you shall speak whatever I command you. Do not be afraid of them for I am with you to deliver you, says the Lord."[1] I had not heard of the prophet Jeremiah at this time in my life, but obviously, Ross had. As I look back now, I wonder if this was God's call to me to go into the ministry. There is no way that I can even begin to compare myself to Jeremiah. He was a tower of faith who took on the political powers of his day and prevailed. I haven't come close to that. Yet, I know that God calls us in the most peculiar ways. There is the story of another prophet, Elijah, who was told to go and stand on a mountain (Horeb) because the Lord was going to pass by. There was a great wind, so strong it was breaking up rocks, and then there was an earthquake followed by fire. But the Lord did not appear in any of these; rather it was in the still small voice, the sound of sheer silence that Elijah saw the Lord[2]—the still small voice of a pastor who said, "God will teach you how to teach." A call to teach Sunday School was nothing compared to the call to be a prophet to the nations, but then again, it was just as scary.

I wasn't about to let Reverend Greek pass off the responsibility of teaching kids who were not much younger than I without some help. I made an appointment to talk with him about teaching. The first lesson I was to teach was about Moses and the Exodus from Egypt. I had seen the movie *The Ten Commandments* the year before. I was impressed with how Charlton Heston, who played Moses, changed in physical appearance when he came down from the mountain after God had given him the commandments. He had an iridescent glow about him that made his whole body look as if it was encased in a halo. I was also impressed with the way the sea parted. Walls of water, hundreds of feet high on both sides, allowed dry land to appear so the Israelites could cross over in safety. When the Egyptians tried to pass through the sea, the waters fell back on them, drowning them all.

"So tell me, Reverend Greek, how do I teach this?"

"For one thing, Walter, you need to realize that this movie got it all wrong. A few years ago, I was part of a group of Jewish, Catholic, and

---

1. Jer 1:4–8.
2. 1 Kgs 19:11–18.

Protestant religious leaders and Biblical scholars C.B.DeMille, the producer of the movie, called together. He showed part of the film that had been made and wanted to know our reaction. We all told him that he was wrong. The waters probably didn't part as dramatically as he portrayed, and the children of Israel probably only numbered six hundred to a thousand instead of the thousands shown in the movie. DeMille was upset with our response and said, 'Well, I'm going to make the movie any damn way I please.'"

"Well, what do I teach?"

"You teach them the truth. God did a great thing on that day. God created the laws of nature, which meant that the waters instead of parting probably receded because it was low tide, and when the Egyptians came through the tide had come back in. Here was God using the laws of his own creation to save his people, and it is the greatest event in what we call the Old Testament. It's a resurrection event. The people were facing death and God rescued them from death, just as God brought back from the dead his own son, Jesus Christ."

I didn't sleep well the Saturday night before my first experience as a teacher. I felt ill prepared to teach kids. I didn't know how to maintain class control. But the thing that bothered me the most was that I didn't know what I believed. I knew I believed in God, but why, I don't know. I had gone to Sunday School whenever my parents got me there, and I was even confirmed in the Congregational Church of Manhasset, New York, when I was fourteen, which was, if my memory serves me right, a twelve week course of study of the major beliefs of the Christian faith. I couldn't connect the words with my life. We were taught that baptism was the sign and seal of the promises of God. A sign and seal? Does someone stamp something on your forehead; no one ever did that to me and I didn't remember my baptism. And what are the promises of God? We were also taught that Jesus atoned for our sins. What's a sin? Going against God. How do I know I am going against God? And what does it mean to atone? I would learn what this word meant in seminary but at the age of fourteen, when I was confirmed, it seemed like a foreign language. I couldn't understand that if God loved me, why my parents couldn't patch up their differences and have a good marriage. I couldn't understand why if God was so powerful he let other kids in school bully and ridicule me, or why God couldn't have given me some athletic ability. But what I do remember is that I felt safe in church. The pastor who taught the confirmation class knew my name and he was always glad to see me. I couldn't wait to get to church to see him. No one in church ridiculed me for being small or for not understanding everything. Adults talked to me and congratulated me when I was confirmed. I may not have known what I was doing, but I learned that Confirmation was important. Reverend Greek's asking me to teach was the first time an adult needed me. I wasn't feeling too needed in my family at that time, but the church needed me, and I needed to be needed. I didn't know what I believed when I walked into that classroom, but I knew I was accepted.

Since I didn't know how to teach, I thought I would just tell the class what Reverend Greek had told me. All the Sunday school classes gathered in the parlor for opening exercises where the Sunday School Superintendent, Peter Haslund, a tall Scandinavian, who was a year older than I was, led us in the singing of two hymns, made announcements, and dismissed us to our classes with prayer. I was grateful for these gatherings because they took up fifteen minutes of my forty-five minute class time. My classroom was nine feet long and seven feet wide. There were solid oak doors at both ends of the room. The side walls were mostly glass—one side looking out onto the street and the other with a view into the semi-circular sanctuary. In the middle of the room, was an old wood, light maple table. Rusty, metal folding chairs surrounded it, creating the teaching area. There were three boys and two girls in the class. I started by having each student read part of the Exodus story aloud. By the time we finished reading the story, I had killed sufficient time so that I didn't have to say much. I started telling them what Reverend Greek had told me, sans the C.B. Demille incident, which I thought they wouldn't understand. When I explained that the Egyptians probably sank in the new wet sand of the tide coming back in, one of the boys said, "Oh, they got stuck in the mud." The other kids started laughing and repeating what this kid had said with one addition. "They got stuck in the mud. They got stuck in the mud. Hooray for God." It sounded like a chant at a sports event. That morning, everyone in the church heard about the Egyptians getting stuck in the mud, and I had my first experience with a show off kid who liked to draw attention to himself and was not beyond disrupting the class to do so. Reverend Greek said to me later, "I hear Pharaoh and his chariots got stuck in the mud." Then he let out one of his big belly laughs and said, "You did just fine, they got the message."

I continued teaching Sunday School and every week I went to see Reverend Greek for my lesson on the next Bible story. One day, there was a new book on the table. As we sat for my lesson, he said, "I bought this for you. It's the Westminster Study Bible." He showed me the articles on the Bible, the introductions to each book, and the maps that were developed by Biblical scholars. "It will help you to understand the Bible, and I want you to bring it with you for our weekly sessions." I was in awe of the book. I hadn't realized there was so much written on the Bible. As Reverend Greek continued to walk my way through my new Bible, I began to realize he had spent his own money on this book. That must have been a financial strain for him since he was paid a salary that was just above the poverty line. But I guess it was like his tooth—I needed the Bible more than he needed the money. I found out a week later that no one else got a Bible—he bought it just for me. Our relationship was special—he was a man, and I needed a male figure in my life—but he was also a man who thought that I was important. That summer, when I got home around midnight from working at Ralph's, I spent an hour or two reading the Bible. By the end of the summer, I had read through the entire Bible.

It was fascinating to see how the Bible was organized. Reading it from cover to cover is not like reading a novel or a history book. The Bible is not organized in chronological order and even within a book material from several centuries may appear. Ross taught me about the Documentary Hypothesis of the Pentateuch—the first five books of the Bible commonly ascribed to Moses as its author. Moses couldn't have written all five books because they record his death, and so others probably had a hand in it. Those others, it is thought, were groups of writers called the Jahwist, Elohist, Priestly, and Deuteronomist, the latter found mostly in the book of Deuteronomy. They were the legal people who were concerned about the laws that the people of God had to follow. The Jahwist saw God as the great, almighty God who was unable to be touched by human hands. The Elohist emphasized the God who was close to us as a mother suckling her infant at her breast. The Priestly writers were more concerned with the rules and order of worship, which may explain why in one part of the Flood story, God tells Noah to bring into the ark two pair of every animal and a few verses later tells him to bring in seven pair. Obviously, it took one pair to procreate, but there was also the need to have enough animals for sacrifices, which would have been the Priestly concern—thus the need for seven pair. Understanding the Bible was like solving a big mystery, only this mystery was thousands of years old. I felt like I was in conversation with people who lived long before me. They were sharing how they came to know God and how they determined what God wanted them to do. I was, also, amazed at how much of the Bible I could understand without knowing all the intricate details. It was as if the Bible was interpreting itself. Later, when I was in seminary, I would learn that one of the doctrines that came out of the Protestant Reformation (those churches who broke away from the Roman Catholic Church in the sixteenth century) was that the Bible interpreted itself. Having a good background in Biblical scholarship was important, but it was also important to meet the Bible face-to-face and let it speak to you.

Soon, I wasn't just seeing Reverend Greek for my weekly sessions. Since the church was on the way home from school, I would stop by and talk with him, usually for an hour at a time. I learned that I could say anything to him and he never reacted negatively.

"I'm not sure about this God," I said. "I mean, how do I know he exists? You say he does, others say he does, but I can't see or hear him."

"Well, look at the Bible. It took over 1400 years for it to be written down. Now do you think if God didn't exist people would have kept an interest in writing what they knew about God?"

"Yeah, but the Bible is an old book. No one speaks like that today. You don't hear God speaking from the heavens; you don't see miracles happening like they did in the Bible. So how do we believe it?"

"Well, you don't believe in the Bible, Walter. You believe in Jesus Christ; you believe in a person. The Bible is a record of people's experience with God and that is what makes it the word of God. The Bible is never the object of our faith; the Bible opens the door to our faith so that we can believe. Of course, some of the words seem strange but people are telling us how important God was to them. You think about it some more. Take your time. Your journey of faith is just beginning, but don't stop asking questions."

"Okay, if God is there and God is so good, why can't he help my parents so they won't get divorced? Why can't he help my mother see that I need my father, too, and I love them both? Why can't we just be a happy family?"

"I don't know, Walter. I know it's painful. I can't take away your pain, even though I wish I could. But I believe that God loves you and one day God will show you how to overcome your pain. And I know that I love you and you're a valuable member of this church. In fact, the whole congregation loves you, too; they think you're going to make a great contribution to life. You're a great person and you have a lot of love in your heart."

Tears welled up in my eyes. I threw my arms around Reverend Greek's large belly and held him tight, and his arms reached around my back and drew me even closer. I don't know how long we hugged, but I remember feeling that I didn't want this moment to pass; I wanted to hold on to him forever. I felt his strength and faith cover me as if it were encapsulating me into a hard cocoon that would protect me and give me the strength to live my life. I didn't have all my questions answered, and I would face a lot of pain in the coming years, but that day my faith changed. God was no longer distant. God was not someone to be discussed as a philosophical problem. Rather, God was now present with me in the form of this pastor who was holding on to me tightly. I thought God must be like Reverend Greek. In fact, even to this day when I think of what God is like, the image of this dedicated pastor comes immediately to mind.

"You know, I'd like to start calling you Ross, if that's okay with you. I just feel so close to you," I said as we released each other from our hugs.

"Why not, Pole Vaulter? We're colleagues in ministry."

I was at church one day in the summer of 1958 and Ross said that he and his wife Norma wanted us young people to come down to their house for a cookout on Friday. Ross lived twenty-five miles away from Hollywood in Granada Hills. It was a new subdivision and the housing prices there were cheaper than in Hollywood. The church sold the manse, which allowed them to give him enough money to pay the mortgage payments. They did this as a favor to him since his salary was quite low and they wanted him to have a house of his own so that when he retired he would not have the added expense of buying a new house.

"Suppose I pick you and Mark (Dragna) up here at the church about four. Mike and Melodie will be there and so will Peter and Ann. They'll be driving themselves and you and Mark can hitch a ride back with them."

On our way down, Ross started talking to Mark and me about sex. At first, I was uncomfortable. I wondered why he brought the subject up. Was he asking Mark and me to have sex with him? We were alone with him in the car and I didn't know what would happen. Yet, Ross and I had been alone many times and he did nothing. I trusted him. On the other hand, part of my discomfort was talking about sex with another guy in the car. I didn't want to show my ignorance. I had had sex education in the ninth grade and the Congregation Church in Manhasset also had sex education classes for us. While I knew the basics of sex, I was still quite confused by the whole thing. In all these classes, no one mentioned masturbation and I masturbated. I felt guilty for doing it. I convinced myself that my father never did anything like that. Of course, I didn't know how girls masturbated, if they did. When Ross mentioned masturbation, all of my reservations went away. I felt relief. Finally, someone was talking about something I had worried about for the past five years. He told us that there was nothing wrong with masturbating; it's a normal behavior and he thought there was never a man or woman who didn't masturbate. The problem comes in when you masturbate too much. It might indicate that you have some fears associated with sex that would not be healthy, and your sperm does give you energy. If you masturbate too much, you might find yourself tired.

I was frightened to ask, but I knew it was best for me to face the answer. How much is too much? I asked. "I think if you have to do it more than once a day then that's too much." A week later in church, I heard Morrie Dragna, Mark's father, thanking Ross for having this talk with his son and me. I realized then that our parents had asked Ross to teach Mark and me about sex. They were too embarrassed to do it themselves.

Ross' house was a small, 1,300 square foot, ranch style, stucco house on Debra Avenue. I forget what color it was, but when we arrived, Ross started the grill and we grilled hamburgers and hot dogs. In the middle of the dinner table was an angel ornament. There were three angels attached to a turret and four candles, the heat from which made the angels revolve in a circle. As they picked up speed, it was impossible to tell if there were three or four angels.

"Pole vaulter, what say you? How many angels are there—three or four?" Ross said.

"There are three angels," I answered, confidently.

"Count them again."

Sure enough when I counted them, I counted four. "It looks like there are four angels."

"No, there's only three," Ross countered. The others around the table got into the discussion—we couldn't agree.

"Pole vaulter, if you're going to be in the church, you gotta know how many angels there are."

I didn't know what to say. If I said, three, Ross would counter with four, and vice versa. I finally said, "Well, ministers are made to be loved and not understood."

The group erupted in laughter led by Ross' own belly laugh. "You got me there," he said as he continued to laugh. I loved that man. He was always laughing and joking, and being around him made me feel secure. It gave me a glimpse that there was more to life than the life I was living with my parents. But more than anything else, he was a man who loved me just as I was.

The next week I stopped in to see him. "Ross, I've got a problem."

"Oh," he said, as if he knew what was coming.

"I masturbate several times a day."

"Let's talk about it."

Over the course of the year, I told him my deepest, darkest secrets and fears. I shared with him the pain of my life—how I felt my body was being torn apart with the realization that my parents were going to divorce, and how I cowered at my mother's verbal assaults. I was afraid to ask a girl on a date because I thought no one would ever want to go out with me. Ross listened patiently. All I could do was to think about sex and masturbate. He pointed out that my masturbation could easily be caused by the stress and the fears in my life, and it probably relieved the anxiety I was feeling of not being accepted and my parents' situation. "It's not easy, Walter, when your mother is as erratic as she is and you essentially have no father. I'm the closest thing you have to a father." Other than that, I don't remember what else he told me, but he never said that I was bad for masturbating, he never condemned me, and he always told me he loved me. Over the course of the year, the need to masturbate lessened considerably.

It was the same way when I came home from attending a college camp the Synod of Southern California ran every year at Big Bear Lake. I had met a girl there and we got along well. One night, we were in the large assembly hall with a bunch of other students laughing, singing camp songs, and telling jokes. As the night wore on, the group got smaller until we were the only ones left in the room. We sat on a sofa and started to kiss. Soon we were into heavy petting. After realizing how late it was, I walked her back to her cabin and kissed her goodnight. The next morning we didn't know what to say to each other. We were embarrassed at what we had done and were feeling guilty, much like the man and woman in the Garden of Eden who hid themselves from God after eating the forbidden fruit. When I got home, the guilt was too much for me to take so I went to see Ross. I told him everything. He listened quietly.

"Walter, what you're telling me is that you and this girl liked each other. She must have liked you enough to let you touch her and for her to touch you. Why don't you write her a letter and tell how you're feeling, but also tell her how much she meant to you, how much you felt accepted by her, and that you will always remember her."

I wrote the letter and waited for what seemed to be years for a reply. The reply came within the week. She was overjoyed with my letter. She had felt guilty, too. She was happy, however, to know how much she meant to me and told me I meant a lot to her. We corresponded a few times. I would have dated her but she lived sixty miles away. I don't remember her name, but I will never forget the beauty of our relationship, and the wise counsel of a loving pastor.

My meetings with Ross seldom ended without his having something he needed done for the church and asking if I would do it. The city condemned our church building and Ross asked if I would draw up some preliminary plans for a new church. "…we have a girl a few years younger than you who wants to come to church but she is blind and has diabetes. How about you picking her up and taking her home every Sunday . . . we need some help in repairing things around the church. Be here at 9:00 am . . . I think it is time for you to participate in the worship service by the reading the Scriptures." It seemed that I no sooner finished with one thing when Ross had another project for me. However, I wasn't prepared for what was to happen next.

I was working at Barker Brothers, a department store in Hollywood just down the street from what was then the Grauman's Chinese Theater, during the Christmas season gift-wrapping items people had purchased. My workroom was next to the elevator, and one night Howard (I forget his last name) who was an Elder in the church came to visit me. He asked if I would let my name be placed before the congregation for election as an Elder. Elders, in the Presbyterian Church, compose the governing body of the church called the Session. The Session has authority over all aspects of the church. In those days, only more mature men were asked to be an Elder. "People have a lot of respect for you, Walter," he said. "They appreciate all the work you do in the church, and you give them hope for the future of the church. They see God working in you." It was a surreal experience. I liked the sound of the words, but I didn't see how they applied to me. I remember thinking, how can these people like and respect me when I don't like and respect me? As it turned out, they were seeing in me what would take decades for me to see. I was ordained. In the Presbyterian Church (U.S.A.) we ordain people to perform special functions, not to a status. Ministers are ordained to preach the Gospel, administer the Sacraments of Communion and Baptism, and provide pastoral care to congregations. Elders are ordained to oversee the spiritual well-being and the temporal affairs of the congregation, and Deacons are ordained to extend the care and sympathy of Christ to others in need. They often provide food, clothing, and housing to the needy. Even though we are not ordained to a status, it is still a great honor to be ordained, and the ordination lasts as long as you live unless it is taken away from you for some unethical and/or illegal behavior. I hold ordination both as an Elder and Minister of Word and Sacrament. Soon after I was ordained, I was elected as the Clerk of Session—the one who took the minutes at Session meetings, and was the chief corresponding officer of the church, although our small church didn't have that much correspondence. When I went to seminary, one of my professors thought he would meet a little old man instead of a young man who still looked like a teenager, because he saw on my application for admission that I was a Clerk of Session, and at that time, most Clerks of Session were older men.

As I look back on it now, I realize Ross never taught me what the Christian faith was—he showed me. Our little church, which had less than a hundred members, had one of the most dynamic youth ministries I have ever seen in my career. There was only one year that I can remember where we actually had youth group meetings. The rest of the time the eight of us were totally involved in the work of the church—ushering, teaching Sunday School, doing the repairs on the building, and anything else Ross needed done. We learned by doing. Ross showed me the unconditional love of God, and that God calls each of us to a life of service regardless of whatever problems we have. Our task is to figure out what God wants us to do and to do it.

∽

The summer after I failed chemistry, I was talking to Ross in the kitchen of the church after finishing with Vacation Bible School that morning. I was toying with several ideas about what I should study and do for a living now that medicine was out of the picture.

"I could be a teacher, Ross. You taught me to like it. I could teach history—I got a "B" in British History and an "A" in the History of Africa this past year. I could even teach psychology or be a counselor."

After listening to me for awhile, Ross said, "Walter, have you ever thought of being a minister? You would be a good one, and God surely needs good ministers."

"Oh, no," I said. "I don't want to be as poor as you are." I am sure that comment must have hurt him but he didn't let on if it did.

"There's a lot more to life than making money, Walter. Do you want to be rich or do you want to make a significant impact on people's lives? Often, the two don't go together."

"I don't know. All that I know is that I don't want to be a minister."

However, in spite of my protests, I knew then that I would become a minister. It only took a few more months for me to acknowledge that God was calling me to the ministry. Intuitive people can put two and two together and come out with seven. In other words, we take a few facts or experiences and put them together to show us the bigger picture and to figure out what needs to be done. I took my love of Ross, the fact that the people in the church always accepted and valued me, the fact that the work I did in the church gave meaning to my life, and put them all together and felt that God was calling me to the ministry. There was no voice from heaven; no earth shaking experience, just the small voice and the pure love of a dedicated pastor who told me that God needed me. Now, for the hard part—breaking the news to my family.

"What the hell do you mean you want to be a minister?" my mother shouted. "You wanna be poor for the rest of your life? You wanna be like Ross?"

"What's wrong with Ross?" I demanded to know. "He has a powerful ministry."

"Oh, yeah, that little two bit church that will never amount to much. Is that what you want to end up with? This is the stupidest idea you ever had. How can you take care of me in my old age if you're not making any money?"

"We were all hoping you would be a doctor," my grandmother chimed in.

"Well, I didn't do very well in chemistry even when I took it over, and you need a lot of chemistry in medicine."

"If you worked a little harder you could've made it," my mother said.

"All that I know is that I feel that God is calling me to the ministry and I must do what God wants me to do."

"Oh, bullshit. Since when did you become so damn religious?"

At the time I made my announcement, my father was back in New York playing with Lombardo again. My parents weren't divorced yet. But, as I look back on it now it was an unacknowledged separation. My mother wrote to him and told him of my decision and then they talked by phone. After the conversation, my mother told me my father thought it was a stupid idea, too. That summer my father came home and we took a walk. He put his arm around my shoulder.

"Walter, if you want to be a minister that's okay with me, but I want you to be the best."

Aw, geez, I thought, I can do whatever I want, even what God wants me to do, but now I have the burden of having to be the best, too. I'm lucky I am passing my classes in college. I haven't had time to even think about being "the best." I was disgusted with my family. I wanted to tell them to go to hell. I wished to God I wasn't born. Jeremiah, when he was being persecuted for his faithfulness to God, said, "Cursed be the day on which I was born…cursed be the man who brought the news to my father 'A child is born to you,' making him very glad. Let that man be like the cities the Lord overthrew without pity . . ."[3] What is so wrong with me, God, that they can't, just for once, pat me on the back and say, "Good going, Walter?" My mother makes me into nothing—she derides everything I stand for or care about. Why couldn't she have just said, "I had my heart set on you being a doctor, and I'm disappointed. But if you give me some time, I'll get over it." I felt I was living in a vacuum—what little faith my family had, neither helped me prepare for nor supported me in my ministry. If God wanted me to be a minister, I would have to do it on my own, and I was prepared to do that. But the loneliness of the struggle, and knowing that my family thought that being a minister was the last thing anyone should be, created in me ten thousand doubts that are now only disappearing as I near retirement and can look back on my life and realize

---

3. Jer 20:14–16.

that I did what God wanted me to do. Jesus said, "A prophet is not without honor except in his own country and in his own house."[4]

⁓

I entered San Francisco Theological Seminary in August of 1964. The flight from Los Angeles to San Francisco was only forty-five minutes—a half hour less than it took us to get to the airport. My mother flew to San Francisco with me. We left a week before I had to report to seminary since my mother had found out that a dear friend of hers was living in San Mateo. Maggie and Jim Williams were neighbors of my parents when I was born. Their two sons, Ralph and Frank, and I played together as toddlers. My mother had always kept in touch with Maggie. I think they found consolation in each other since both of their husbands supposedly had numerous affairs. Maggie met us at the airport with her daughter, Mitsy, who was born about eight years after I was, so we hadn't met until now. She was a beautiful, precocious girl who liked to come into my room, at night, in her baby doll pajamas and talk to me. To say that I was not sexually attracted to her would be a gross understatement, but I had to remind myself that she was fourteen and I was twenty-two. Maggie was about 5′6" tall, had blond hair and blue eyes, and a good figure. Her voice was deep, somewhat like Lauran Bacall's, which made her sensuous. Her husband Jim who was an engineer, if memory serves me correctly, was on a business trip. We would only get to see him for two days. There was plenty of liquor around the house, and I surmised that Maggie was an alcoholic.

"Hey, Doona, it's good to see you," Ralph and Frank called out as we pulled into the driveway. Ralph was two years older than I was and Frank was a year younger than I was. *Doona* was my old nickname and I hated it. Kids who knew my nickname called me *Doona the Dunce*. I even have trouble writing it now but the story is more important than my need to keep it a secret. The name came from my mother and she never stopped using it until I was into my teens even though she knew it brought on ridicule from other kids. I don't know where the name came from. It was one of my mother's concoctions, and she chose not to explain its origins even though I asked her on several occasions.

Ralph had just gotten out of the army. Both he and Frank were tall and strong. They took me to San Francisco one night. We drove in Ralph's

4. Matt 13:57.

1962 Ford Thunderbird convertible with the top down. The brothers wanted to do a lot of drinking so we ended up at a bar. The bartender carded me but seemed to know the brothers. They ordered beer and whiskey—boiler makers. I ordered what I thought was the least harmful—a rum and coke. I had not consumed any alcohol up until this time, so drinking was a new experience for me. We arrived at the bar at 9:00 pm and left at 2:00 am. As we sat at the bar, I nursed my rum and coke as long as I could before having to order another one. This time, I only ordered coke. Ralph and Frank seemed to down two or three boiler makers every hour. There was an older woman who I guess was about fifty-five. She had black hair, a good figure, and was attractive. She kept her hands mostly on Ralph and every so often would snuggle up to Frank. She didn't pay too much attention to me except at one time she put her arm around my shoulder and drew my head into her shapely breasts and said, "What's the matter, honey, don't you like to drink?" I felt uncomfortable. I was young looking for my age and small in stature, and her arm around me with my lips almost touching her nipples made me think she was treating me as a little boy, which she probably was. I remember making some feeble response. She then went back to caressing Ralph.

I felt out-of-control at the bar. I never liked situations where I thought someone might get me to do things I didn't want to do. I don't like "wheeler dealers"—people who are skilled in talking and thinking fast and have the ease to move in and out of groups of people. I never know if I am getting a good deal or getting shafted—if I'm being told the truth or being used for someone's entertainment. My fear of such situations has led me to shy away from many things such as church politics and arguments. I only get involved when I know my material extremely well. People who have been sexually abused are always sensitive to being controlled by others. Sexual abuse is not about sex, of course, but about domination and control. The adult seeks to control the child by violating the child's private space. That violation makes the child feel he or she has no control over any part of their lives. The child goes through life seeking to control their life and when they meet controlling people, it is hard for them to resist being controlled. The whole situation brings back memories of their abuse when they felt vulnerable. The only way to get out of this situation is to know your material so well that you can withstand any challenge. In a situation where that is not possible, it's best to withdraw. It is a way we have of protecting ourselves.

As I look back on it now, the bar scene helped me to define myself. I couldn't see what was to be gained by sitting at a bar for five hours drinking, having a woman old enough to be your mother trying to seduce you, and then spending the next day in bed recovering from a hangover. I felt I was watching the dance of empty souls wanting to be filled, hoping the next drink would satisfy them, hoping the next caress would bring love, and hoping that their lives were not as meaningless as they felt they were. I don't speak from a position of superiority, however. Thirty years into the future, I would have my own war with alcohol as I tried to fill my own empty life and struggled to find love. The bottle is a great lover at first, but then it becomes a deadly lover. My experience at the bar reinforced Ross' question to me—do you want to be rich or do you want to have a significant impact on peoples' lives? The Williams' were rich. Their ranch style home covered five thousand square feet. One room was dedicated to their regulation size pool table with a slate top and leather pockets, and they had just signed a contract to build a thirty by forty foot swimming pool. I envied them their wealth as I have envied everyone who has wealth throughout my life. I have a lover's anger at the church for the paltry sums it pays to its pastors. The church doesn't think that what we do is worth adequate financial reward.

Once a wealthy farmer in Minnesota said to me, "You ministers don't get paid much but you have other rewards." To which I replied, "Yes, but they don't pay the electric bill." I've helped many people die in peace, comforted their survivors, brought the presence of God to people who were ill and afraid, taught people to be good teachers, counseled with distraught people and brought them hope—what's that worth? But because I don't have to meet a payroll, work like other people do, and am not supposed to worry about earthly things, the church thinks it can justify paying small salaries. The struggle between needing more money and being significant in peoples' lives has always been a conflict for me. But that night I saw something else. The Williams' might have been wealthy, but they were empty. That night, I knew I wanted to make a significant impact on peoples' lives, and it would be that same desire that would lead me out of the pit of alcohol thirty years later.

∽

Before I left for seminary Ross said, "Don't worry about your grades in seminary. There is only one criterion for success—do your classes deepen your personal relationship with Jesus Christ? If they don't, do what you have to do to pass and move on. If they do, study like hell and get the best grade you can. You can get a 'C' in a class, but if it deepens your faith it is worth more than all the "A's" in the world."

The entering class had to arrive on campus a month ahead of the other students for three weeks of intensive Hebrew. There were four hours of class per day and six hours of homework. I did well in Hebrew—much better than I did in any other languages I took in college or high school. Reading from right to left was fascinating, and it was always a challenge to remember to open my Hebrew Bible from what we normally considered the back of the book. As I was learning the language, I came to realize that I was reading words that had been written down three thousand years before I was born. Because the Bible is the story of God's relationship to his people and their struggles to bring God into their lives, I soon came to think of Hebrew as God's language, and that I was in direct conversation with God. God was as accessible to me as my Hebrew Bible.

My first class in seminary was Introduction to the Old Testament, taught by one of the greatest Biblical scholars of the twentieth century, James Muilenburg. By the time, I had Dr. Muilenburg, he was in his mid-70's and had the disheveled look of an Old Testament Prophet. His white, thin hair was never combed mainly because he was always running his hand through his hair as he lectured. His false teeth didn't fit properly, and as he spoke his upper plate would come loose and drop and hit the lower plate, causing a clicking noise. We all knew of Muilenburg's stature as a Biblical scholar and coupled with my thinking that Hebrew was God's language, it didn't take much for me to feel in the presence of God that first semester of seminary. What also impressed me was that what Muilenburg was teaching us, Ross had taught me several years earlier. It was a profound moment for me when I realized the quality of education I had received from Ross before I even decided to be a minister.

Muilenburg was writing a book on the prophet Jeremiah. Everyone knew that when his book was published, all other books on Jeremiah could be discarded. He was by far the world's greatest authority on the book. In my third year of seminary, I took a class on Jeremiah from him. He always taught us in class that the Bible is not meant to be read silently—it is meant to be spoken. The emphasis is always on the spoken word of God—not the written—so when we read the Bible we're to read it out loud. One day, I saw Muilenburg come out of a classroom and take a drink at the water fountain. I went over to him and said, "Dr. Muilenburg, I don't think you should write your book on Jeremiah." He quickly looked up at me with a scowl as water dripped from his lips. "No, Dr. Muilenburg," I continued before he could say anything, "You should tape record it." A big smile came over his face, and he said, as he patted me on my shoulder, "Ah, Mr. Smith, Mr. Smith, you understand, you understand. Bless you, my son." I got an "A" from him in Jeremiah.

Theology was another matter. I had two professors for Introduction to Theology—Arnold Come and Benjamin Reist. I could understand Come—he talked slower and connected all the dots. Reist on the other hand was a fast talker. He even joked on the first day in class that he talked so fast we needed to bring five pencils to class, because if we dropped one and had to pick it up, we would miss three names on the way down and two on the way back up. I was having trouble understanding these new theological terms and Reist wasn't very patient in explaining them. I also felt intimidated being among such great scholars so I tended not to ask questions for fear of being shown to be of inferior intelligence. I was to find out I was not alone. About four weeks into the fall semester, Paul Tillich, one of the great theologians of the twentieth century, came to campus. He was well into his seventies and he sat in a chair on a platform in this large room that held about three hundred people. He spoke for a while and then he asked for questions. Dr. Reist rose. I don't remember his exact question but it went something like this: "Dr. Tillich, in Volume One of your Systematic Theology, chapter two, page 63, paragraph two, and line four you say such and such. Then in Volume Three, chapter four, page 142, paragraph three, and line two you say such and such. This appears to me as a contradiction, could you please explain what you're saying?" Tillich looked at Reist and said, "Well, Doctor, if you just read it yesterday and don't understand it, how do you expect me to explain it when I wrote it over five years ago?" The audience erupted into laughter, and I fell in love with Paul Tillich. Regardless of his great mind, he was willing to admit he didn't understand it all, even now. Those of us who were in Introduction to Theology were overjoyed—we weren't the only ones who didn't understand what we were learning—maybe even our esteemed professor didn't understand either.

That first semester of seminary was not only intellectually challenging but also physically and mentally challenging. My parents had had a bitter divorce three years earlier. My mother had drafted me into her service by having me call her attorney while she was at work to ask a question or provide him with information, going to court with her, and reading the private investigator's report on my father's adultery, which was to prove to me that my father was no good. It also gave her all the grounds she needed to secure a divorce, with alimony, to demand that I not be like my father, and to prove it to her by giving her my full allegiance, which meant not having contact with him or ever talking about him. I was angry with my father for what he did to my mother and so her demands were easily met, at first. My mother told me after the divorce that she needed me more than ever, and that I was now the "man" of the house. We owned a house in the San Fernando Valley, which we were renting out. It became my responsibility to make sure it was rented, to deal with the real estate agent and the tenants.

One day a sheriff came to our house and served a summons on my mother to appear in court to explain why she had not appeared when instructed to for a speeding ticket. My mother had not gotten a speeding ticket. We had, however, sold a car and we surmised the new owner had not registered the car in his name and it was he who got the ticket. My mother said, "I can't handle this, you do it for me, Walter." I collected the documentation on our sale of the car and wrote the judge a letter. I had my mother sign it. A week or so later, a letter from the judge arrived saying that he had dismissed all charges. I showed it to my mother. "Oh, you're a wonderful son. What would I do without you?" Her praise made me feel good, but it also made me feel that I could never leave my mother.

I felt guilty that first semester in seminary. It was the first time I lived away from home. I was homesick, and worried about how my mother was going to survive without me. My stomach started hurting. It felt hard and twisted as if someone was wringing it as if they were wringing the water out of a wet towel. I couldn't eat—the food felt like it didn't want to go down. I lay in bed for several days missing some of my classes. I made an appointment with a doctor. His office was two miles away, but I couldn't find anyone to drive me, so I walked. During the walk, the pain went away. The doctor was compassionate and the way he touched me during the examination was comforting. He was gentle and just asked many questions in a low, reassuring voice. He gave me a prescription for Valium and suggested I do more walking. He was sure that, in the near future, the pain would go away. It did.

At Thanksgiving, I went home. The trip, which normally took about six hours, seemed to take six days. I couldn't wait to get back into my house and be with my mother. She met me at the airport. I was so glad to see her that I gave her a big hug and kiss. As the car pulled into the driveway, I ran into the house. I was not prepared for the feeling I had as I came through the door. All of a sudden, I felt I was in a strange house. While things looked familiar, they were no longer part of me. It was as if I no longer lived there. I wanted to turn around and go back to the seminary. I was disappointed that my return trip was five days away.

If the study of the Old Testament was my affirmation of being close to God, and the study of theology raised questions in me about God, then the study of the New Testament was the challenge to my faith. I could easily accept the fact that the Old Testament contained many places that contradicted each other. The Biblical writers were not so much interested in the facts as they were with what they meant. But in the New Testament, I assumed, for some reason, that everything that was recorded was what Jesus said even though the New Testament doesn't agree on all the facts either—just compare the birth story of Jesus in Matthew with the one in Luke. But it was also at the time when the influence of Rudolph Bultmann, a German New Testament scholar, was high with our seminary professors alluding to his works and requiring us to read some of them. Bultmann, and I am not going to give a full representation of his thought, postulated that Jesus probably said very little of what is recorded in the Gospels— that they were really the creation of the early church who wrote them in a particular historical context to drive home a point about who Jesus was. For him, the facts of the faith weren't important; what was important was whether or not you believed. Bultmann's ideas have gone by the wayside today, but his thinking left its mark on me. If you followed Bultmann completely, you could easily discount the New Testament as a serious work. I was taught in Old Testament classes that God was a God of history and worked out the salvation of the created order through historical events. If there wasn't much to the factual history of the New Testament, then how can we accept the New Testament in the same light as the Old? But more importantly, Bultmann led me to doubt if Jesus Christ was real.

During that first year, I also began to wonder why I was in seminary, and if the ministry was what I wanted. I was coming to understand my need to please others even when it went against what I wanted to do. Part of that came from my mother who taught me early on that pleasing her brought rewards while not pleasing her could make my life miserable. But I also felt that my need to please had been with me since birth. Pleasing is an important part of ministry. It has made my work go smoother, and I have had fewer conflicts with people than others who have a more competitive nature and insist on their own way. The problems came when I did things I didn't want to do, and denied who I was and what I stood for. So, was I in seminary because I wanted it, or was it because I wanted to please Ross? He was the father I never had and I didn't want to lose him. I noticed the other young people in the church who chose different careers were not as close to him as I was. They didn't speak the same language or share the same values as did Ross and I. Of course, he loved the other young people, but I had the feeling he loved me a little more. Our relationship was unique, and I wanted to keep it that way.

However, as much as I loved Ross, there were some cracks in our relationship. When I shared with him that I wanted to be a minister, two years before I graduated from college, he was pleased and thought that I had made a wise choice. We had prayer in which he asked God to guide me and make me into the minister God wanted me to be. He then told me that I shouldn't worry about paying for seminary. He was sure the church would give me at least $500.00 a year for my tuition and that the seminary would fund the rest. Seminary education cost about $1,500 per year, then. Of course, I would have to work and contribute some myself. I was overjoyed because I didn't know how I would pay for additional schooling. In the spring of my senior year in college, I made application to San Francisco Theological Seminary. On the financial part, was a question about how much money my local church would give toward my expenses. I went to Ross believing that he would reaffirm what he had told me two years earlier. Instead, he said, "Nothing. We can't afford a single dime toward your education. You'll have to do it on your own." I was stunned. His words seemed sharp. I didn't say anything, but I wondered if my relationship with him was all that special. I felt abandoned. Of course, he was telling me the truth. As an Elder in the church, I knew we had little money, but I thought that Ross would get it some way. I got through seminary with little debt thanks to other congregations. But the lack of support from my own church and my family's reaction to my wanting to be a minister gave me a sense of loneliness that was deep and painful.

On Easter, 1965, I went to church with a few of my friends. It was a small congregation. The people recognized us instantly as seminary students and greeted us warmly. The Pastor started the service by saying, "Jesus Christ is risen." The congregation responded, "He is risen indeed." The organist started playing, *Jesus Christ is Risen Today*, and we all stood and joined our voices together making a joyful noise unto the Lord. I found it difficult to sing the hymn. The words seemed strange and foreign. The resurrection, which I had never doubted before, now seemed implausible. If the Gospels were a creation of the early church, how did I know that the early church didn't concoct the story of the resurrection? I didn't pay attention to the service or the pastor's sermon. I sat with my head bowed during most of the service, which was not the proper position for a service of joy and celebration. I prayed repeatedly, "God, I believe you exist, but I don't know if I believe in this Jesus guy of yours. I don't even know if I should be in seminary or go into the ministry. I think you made a mistake with me. If you want me to be a minister, then you better make it clear to me or else I'm out of here."

After my first year in seminary, I returned home. I went to see Ross. The Hippie movement was in full swing and being located on Sunset Boulevard, the church was right in the center of the activity. Ross reached out to the Hippies and started drug rehabilitation programs, and helped these social rebels to channel their creative energies into summer programs for inner-city children, collecting food for the hungry, some of which were themselves, and learning how to reduce the neighbors' suspicion of people who wore long hair and sandals and didn't bathe. Of course, in the process, Ross lost many of the traditional members of the church. Now he was the beloved pastor of the hippies and would be recognized as a great civic leader in years to come. He told me what had happened in the time I was gone. "Pole Vaulter," he said, "You've missed it all. You're just up there in seminary studying, while the real action is going on down here. You got to get with it, man—God is here, not up there." Again, I was stunned. It was as if he was saying that what I was doing in seminary wasn't important. What was important was his ministry and that's where God was working. I told him how he made me feel, but he just said, "I've got other things to deal with now." I felt even lonelier, and I doubted if seminary was where God wanted me to be.

Arnold Come offered a course in the second quarter of the 1965–66 school-year entitled, *The Uniqueness of the Christian Faith*, and I took it.

By the description of the course, I thought this class would help me with my doubts. I wouldn't be disappointed. Come was a tall, thin man with an oval face and a bald head. He spoke quietly, slowly, and reassuringly. He devised the class as an exploration of what the great religious leaders of the church said about Jesus throughout the centuries. As we moved through the years, I saw people of great intellect, such as Augustine, Aquinas, Luther, Calvin, and others proclaim their faith in Jesus Christ as the Son of God who was crucified and raised from the dead. Salvation comes through our faith in Jesus Christ, who has the power to redeem any life. This was no more evident than in the life of Augustine who, in his early years, was a drunk, sexually promiscuous, and had a child out-of-wedlock. He converted to Christianity when he saw how empty his life was, and went on to be the second greatest theologian in the church next to Paul. Much to his credit, he acknowledged that he had fathered a child, claimed him as his son, and provided for him.

I was impressed by the fact that people over the course of the centuries, who never met each other, could proclaim a common faith in this man Jesus. There must have been something to this Jesus for these people to say essentially the same thing about him. Coupling that with the fact that many of these people suffered and even died for their faith in Jesus Christ made me realize that this Jesus was more than just another good person. During the course, we also talked about Good Friday when Jesus was crucified and his disciples ran away and hid because they were afraid the Romans would crucify them, too. Yet, when they were told by the women that Jesus had been raised, they came out of hiding and proudly proclaimed they were his disciples and began teaching, preaching, and healing in Jesus' name. Such a change could not have occurred if the resurrection had not happened. While the church has never been perfect, it has proclaimed its faith in Jesus Christ for twenty centuries. If Jesus was a phony, if they found the body, the church could not have kept up the façade. It would have soon disappeared.

Come's course deepened my faith by helping me to see that it just wasn't Ross and me and a few others trying to live out our faith, but that I was a part of a movement that went beyond the church and me. I was a part of something that began before creation itself and would never come to an end. I was a part of the greatest movement the world has ever seen; a movement that has had its dark moments, but has never been defeated. It reminds me of deep-sea fishing. When I drop my line into the water and feel that sixteen ounce sinker hit the floor of the ocean, six hundred feet below, I feel that I am connected to everything that is below me, above me, around me, in me, and outside of me. I'm connected to the entire cosmos; I'm connected to God. I don't exist as a separate entity. My existence is part of those who have gone before me, dwell on this earth with me now, and will come after me. The late Swiss psychiatrist, Carl Jung, believed that we are born with all of the knowledge and experiences of those who have gone before us, and in our lives we are endowing future generations with the knowledge and experiences we have acquired. John, the writer of the Gospel, views our present life as a part of eternal life. We are living in eternity now, death is a path we travel to make that eternity permanent. So, what I am doing now is not just living. I am participating in creation itself. I am participating in the life, power, love, redemption, and salvation of God as revealed in Jesus Christ. My life now had a purpose. It just wasn't about Ross and me, it was about God.

I remembered my prayer on Easter Sunday and realized that God had answered it by leading me to Arnold Come. The faith was real, and I felt the best place for me to express what I was learning and experiencing was in the church. By the end of the class, I knew God wanted me to be a minister. I wasn't pleasing anyone but God. I forget what grade I received, but it was the course that put my faith back together after it had been torn apart and tested. It was, for me, the class that most deepened my faith in Jesus Christ, and according to Ross, was worth all the "A's" in the world.

It was a hot, unusually clear Los Angeles Sunday afternoon on July 9, 1967 when I was ordained to the office of Minister of Word and Sacrament by the Presbytery of Los Angeles at the West Hollywood Presbyterian Church. The old church had been torn down several years before, and the new church was composed of two white, single floor stucco rectangular buildings joined by a canopy walkway that lacked the stature, grace, and dignity of the old pink church where the hand from heaven pulled me into its presence. One building housed the sanctuary while the other the church office and fellowship hall. The Presbytery, which is like a diocese, forms a commission to ordain candidates for the Ministry, and Ross headed the Commission. Other ministers on the Commission were Eduardo Bodipo Malumba, a seminary classmate from Nigeria; Russ Prentiss, another minister who was on the Examination Committee of the Presbytery; and Jim McDill, whose wife came from Scotland where I would serve a church in the coming year. Elders were Morrie Dragna, and my friend Mike McElliott. Linda McKaughan, a woman I was dating at seminary, played the organ, and my former girlfriend, Pam Hotchkiss, with whom I was still in love, came to share the joy of the occasion.

The worship service began with the Commission members walking down the short center aisle of the white painted sanctuary, that seated about a hundred people, and taking its place in the chancel area. Windows on both sides of the chancel were clear glass. The reason was that the world could always look in and see what we were doing because the church shouldn't hide anything. I sat in the front pew. The service was simple, and at the appropriate time, I was called forward and asked the ordination questions. After answering them in the affirmative, I was asked to kneel. Ross and the members of the Commission placed their hands on my head, and Ross led the congregation in the ordination prayer. Six hands on my head felt heavy—heavy, I thought of the burden I was taking on—heavy, the burden of getting to this time and place. Oh God, will I have the strength to serve you as you want? After the prayer, I was led up to the chancel area where Ross delivered his charge to me. I don't remember much of what he said but I do remember how he finished.

"Walter, to thine own self be true. Stand up and be counted or sit down and be counted out."

A reception was held after the service. My mother was aglow and proud she was the mother of the one being ordained. Perhaps she had reconciled herself to her son's lowly estate. Since my parents were divorced, my father, who was living in New Jersey, thought it best not to come. By now, I was used to the fact that he was never present at things that were important to me, but I still felt abandoned, and it hurt. I couldn't understand why my parents couldn't have put aside their differences just for once, for me. Church members expressed their admiration for me and wished me the best in Scotland, and the Hippies gave me hugs, kisses, and flowers. When I got home, I read over the guest book. People had not only signed their names but had also written in their best wishes. Ross had written, "Best to the best."

I wept.

7

Dad, No Dad

*"Children, obey your parents in the Lord, for this is right.
Honor your father and mother—this is the first commandment
with a promise: so that it may be well with you and you may live long
on the earth. And, fathers, do not provoke your children to anger,
but bring them up in the discipline and instruction of the Lord."*

EPH 6:1–4

ON AN EARLY DAY in May, 1962, at San Fernando Valley State College in Northridge, California it was warm and sunny, but my body told me it was cold and cloudy. I was a 20 year-old junior majoring in Psychology and at 4:30 pm, I left the school to travel to Beverly Hills in our family's 1954 powder blue Cadillac to pick up my mother from Saks Fifth Avenue, where she worked as a sales woman. As I drove out of the parking lot, I noticed the sun beginning its initial descent, casting a golden brown glow over the mountains that were behind me and cool green shadows over the mountains before me, the ones I had to traverse to reach Beverly Hills. My mother hated it if I was late, so I allowed myself an hour to get there just in case there was a traffic tie up. I arrived fifteen minutes early and parked near the store. While waiting for her, I checked the tires, opened the hood, and looked at the engine. What I was looking for I don't know; I wouldn't be able to tell if anything was wrong unless I saw a gaping hole in the water hose. I must have opened and closed the hood two or three times while waiting. I was anxious—I didn't know how I would tell her that I received a letter from my father a few days earlier in response to a letter I wrote to him.

My parent's marriage would end in divorce later that year. My mother sued for divorce, and the judgment went against my father on the grounds of adultery. He was having an affair with my aunt (my mother's brother's wife). Actually it was more than an affair; they were married before the divorce was final, making my father a bigamist.

My parents had a big fight the year before. My father came home for the summer in 1961 from working in New York with Guy Lombardo. For the previous year he sent my mother $900.00 a month and was shocked to find out there wasn't any of that money left. He left that September to go back to work with Guy, but he never sent anymore money.

I saw my mother exit the store on time. Seldom did she stay over closing time unless she had a favorite customer who was buying a lot of clothes.

"So what's new?" she asked as I opened the car door for her.

My mouth was dry. I could hardly speak. I knew I had to tell her about the letter. My grandmother knew I received the it, and it was only a matter of time before she would tell my mother, and I had a better chance of survival if the news came from me rather than from Nana.

"I got a letter from Dad the other day," I said.

My mother didn't respond. The fifteen-minute trip home was made in silence. There was little traffic to impede our way, but my insides were tied up in knots making each red light and each step on the brake pedal feel like one more stay of execution, which I knew would come eventually. No matter what I did, it was wrong. I knew I had dealt a serious blow to my mother, but I was so elated to receive a letter from my father saying how happy he was to hear from me and that he hoped we could keep in touch regardless of what was happening between him and my mother. If I pleased my mother, I displeased my father and vice versa. I was being torn between two people I loved. It was ripping me apart inside. My mother got out of the car and slammed the door as soon as I pulled into the driveway. I followed her into the single story bungalow we were renting. My grandmother was sitting in the deep, blue, high-armed chair that had become hers over the years by default. My mother turned to me and yelled,

"Who the hell do you think you are going behind my back and writing your father?" Her anger matched the heat of the sun.

"I need him. He's my father."

"Oh bullshit. You're twenty years old. Can't you see what that son of a bitch has done to me? How can you have any need for a man who has treated me that way? You don't give a shit about me. You wouldn't do this if you loved me."

"I do love you and I love Dad," I said.

"Impossible," my mother snapped back. "How could you after he left me for that slut, my own brother's wife. Do you know how much he's hurt me and you want to love him?" Usually she would be in tears when she told me how I disappointed her. But, now, she was too angry.

As I stood before my mother, I felt naked. It was as if she were lashing me with a whip and the lashes were coming fast and furious. The air was being sucked out of my lungs and my stomach felt like it was caving in. I was in pain and breathless at the same time. I could hardly talk, much less shed the tears that were filling the giant hole in my gut. My mother didn't believe me, and she questioned my love.

Where are you, God, when I need you? I don't care if my parents can't get along, but why can't you at least let me have parents who will allow me to love them? I thought. I finally caught my breath enough to say, "I can't help what Dad has done. All I know is I need you both."

"Oh, bullshit. He hasn't done a goddamn thing for you. I did everything for you. I took you to scouts and school events. I was there for you. He didn't care about you. You want him, then go live with him and get the hell out of my house. As far as I'm concerned, you're no longer my son."

What made her onslaught even more painful was the fact that she was right. My father missed most of the important events in my life. The damnable thing about my mother was that in her rightness she forced me to acknowledge the pain of my father's abandonment. She caused me to doubt not only his love but God's love, and created in me thousands of doubts about my own worth as a person who chose to love a man who gave me no reason to do so except that he was my father.

My thoughts went back to the time I had a workbench made for him in 1955 when I was thirteen years old and we were living in Roslyn, New York. He always wanted a workbench that he could hang on the garage wall so he could lower it when he wasn't using it and still allow space for the car. While he was away for three months on a musical tour, I collected various pieces of 'two by fours' and began to frame the workbench. The resulting frame sagged in the middle. One end was three feet wide and the other three and a half feet wide. I threw the frame down in disgust. A carpenter, working at our neighbor's house, had been observing my labor.

"What are you trying to make?" he asked.

"A workbench for my father. I want to surprise him when he comes home."

"What do you want it to look like?" I showed him the plans. "That's a pretty good idea you have there. I have some extra wood. Let me go get it and see what we can do." Within a few minutes, the workbench was completed.

"How does that look?" he asked.

"It's perfect. It's just what I wanted. How come I couldn't do that?"

"It's taken me years to learn how to do this, son," he said. "You're just beginning. You'll be able to do it one day, too."

"Thanks. How much do I owe you?"

"How much money you got?" he asked.

"Seventy-five cents," I said.

"Would twenty-five cents be a fair price?"

"Oh, yes sir."

When my father came home, I took him out to the patio where the workbench was covered with a bedspread.

"Take the bedspread off, Dad." He took it off and looked at the workbench.

"It's your workbench, Dad. It's what you always wanted. I had it made for you."

"It's nice," he said. "Let's cover it up. It might rain."

"When do you want to put it up, Dad?"

"I don't know," he said. "It might be too heavy to hang on the wall. We'll see." Then he went back into the house. I went to my room. As I look back, that carpenter, whose name I didn't know, was more of a father to me than my own.

~

My father never told me much about his childhood except that he was born and named Walter Claude Smith in Bethlehem, Pennsylvania, on August 12, 1911. He was the only child of Claude and Laura Smith. What I knew about his childhood came from my mother, grandmother, and other relatives. Anna, one of my father's cousins who lived next door to him, told me that she would often hear him screaming as the straps of the Cat-o-Nine Tails seared his bare flesh. "You could hear him screaming two blocks away," she said. Roger, Anna's husband, said that Laura and Claude were crazy. Charlie, another cousin, told me that they both took trumpet lessons, but it was obvious that my father was the superior trumpeter. Charlie was amazed that my father did so well in music because often the beatings my father received left his nose and ears bloody. "You'd think he be deaf," Charlie said. In fact, my father didn't have a hearing problem. What he did have was almost perfect pitch.

By the time he was eighteen, my father was playing trumpet professionally. He started out playing for college dances at Lehigh University in Bethlehem. When he married my mother in 1931, he moved to Brooklyn and got into the New York music scene. I remember my father telling me that there were twenty thousand musicians in New York City around 1950, yet only two thousand had full-time music jobs. My father was never without full-time work until he left Lombardo a second time in his early sixties. I assumed that meant my father was a good musician. However, he complained that Lombardo's music was something that any novice musician could play. "There was just no challenge to it," he said. So was my father good or just good enough to play simple music? Other musicians told me he was good, but it wasn't until I contacted a man who knew my father well that I got insight into how good my father really was and what being a musician meant to him.

Edward Cardelli responded to an advertisement I placed in the New York Musicians Union newspaper trying to locate anyone who knew my father. In January 1999, seven years after my father's death, I was able to talk with him on the phone. Cardelli told me that my father was a natural with music. "Other musicians would brag about how good they were, but not your father. He didn't have to. Everyone knew how good he was as soon as they heard him play. He could play a thousand songs without a sheet of music. You have to in this business. When you're playing a date (musical engagement) and someone asks you to play a song, you can't take time rummaging through your music to find it. But only the good ones could do it."

By now my heart was beginning to burst with pride. I had never heard anyone talk in such glowing terms about my father. It was as if Cardelli was affirming me as he affirmed my father. I wanted to know what a musician's life was like, and Cardelli did not disappoint me.

"Musicians are wonderful people. A good musician can be anything: a doctor, lawyer, or an actor; they're dedicated and artistic people. Where can you find work that allows you to dress up in tuxedos, get to know important people, play in some of the nicest places in the world, eat good food, and make beautiful music? Your dad could make beautiful music. In fact, his favorite song was the *Battle Hymn of the Republic*, and boy could he play it."

Artistic? Able to make beautiful music? My atheistic father's favorite song, *The Battle Hymn of the Republic?* These were words I never associated with my father. The father I knew was a bland, passionless individual who hardly laughed or gave any indication that anything excited him. As Cardelli talked, I absorbed his words deep into the marrow of my bones. It was almost as if his words were melting my thoughts of my father and pouring them into a new vessel of understanding and empathy. Musicians weren't the lifeless creatures I often thought they were; they were life-giving artists with great passion for creating beautiful sounds. Surely there must have been a down side to this life? What was it I wanted to know? What hope did they have?

"Musicians don't have hope," Cardelli said. "Only great composers have hope." He went on to explain that musicians never dwell on the future because they don't know where their next job will come from, and they fear they will be unable to take care of their families not only financially, but also with their presence because they have to travel so much of the time. "It was why your Dad stuck with Lombardo even though the music was bland—it was permanent work. Very few bands worked as much as Lombardo."

I began having a deeper appreciation for my Dad. Here was a great musician who was stuck playing kid's music. I must admit I still like Lombardo's music even though I know it has little character or depth. But it's the kind of music that when I'm dancing with someone I feel close to them, almost as if we are one. It is soft music that connects me to others, and makes me feel part of that great landscape called humanity. But it's also music that my Dad is making. I can't hear his trumpet per se, unless he has a solo, but I know it's there, and as I join with another person in a dancing embrace I bring my life to that experience; I give my partner the fabric from which my life was woven.

No wonder my father couldn't be excited about his music with me—it wasn't exciting to him. Every night he went to work, he had to suppress his skill as a trumpeter and listen to the same music repeatedly just to put food on the table and a roof over our heads all while my mother was complained that we didn't have enough money. He must have felt downtrodden and defeated, probably just as he felt as the cat-o-nine tails ripped across his flesh as a child. I wonder what it was like for him to be born only to realize a few years later that much of the world was against him and he would never fulfill what God called him to be.

Then I realized that I have never shared with my boys my love for the ministry. Mostly what they have gotten are my complaints. They never saw in me the fulfillment I have of being with people in their deepest hour of need. They never saw how terrifying and at the same time exhilarating it was for me to prepare and preach a sermon. To think that I had been entrusted by the church and by God to speak the word of God is at once a great honor and a great responsibility. For who could ever have the audacity to think that they could ever speak for God, yet that is what I am called to do. On the other hand, the ministry is also a dull and boring routine. Cutting and pasting the church bulletin together, running a projector, cleaning out the coffee pot, answering simple calls, opening and closing the church, and attending endless meetings that often go nowhere except to give the attendees an opportunity for socialization often define the life of a minister more than the times we are in true ministry. I often wondered why there were no good television shows about the life of a minister, but when I think of my life as a minister, there's not that much excitement. Ministry takes place over years and what seems to be many inconsequential conversations. However, when those people with whom you've only talked about the weather lose a family member or suffer a debilitating disease, they cling to your every word, hold you tightly in their arms, soak your shoulder with their tears, and tell you that they couldn't get through this without you.

My father's quietness, however, was disturbing to me as a child. I may not have shared my joy of the ministry with my sons, but at least I talked to them. I couldn't get through to my father. I never felt connected to him, and with a child's mind I thought it was my fault. If I were a better son, he would talk to me. If I were a better son, he wouldn't drink so much. My father never raised his hand to me, although my mother told me of the time he hit the back of my legs with a leather belt when I was about three and my mother told him never to do that again. And he was never verbally abusive. One day when I was about seven, he took me aside and quietly said that he did not like my picking my nose and eating it. That was not healthy to do and it did not look nice. Would I please stop it? I did. A few years later, I told him and my mother that I did not like being called *Butch* or *Doona*. My father stopped immediately, and started calling me, *Walter*. It took another three years of my complaining for my mother to stop.

I was never afraid to be in my father's presence. What I feared was the unknown. I didn't know who my father was, what he thought, what he hoped for, what he was like when he was a child. I didn't even know if he liked me. As a child, I wanted him to hold me, kiss me, and tell me he was proud of me. He never did. I felt adrift with my father. I didn't have a place to drop my anchor and feel secure. While I didn't think about it then, later in life I was angry with him. Where was he when my mother was showing her power over me in front of other women as she adjusted my underwear? Why wasn't he the one to take me to the doctor about my un-descended testicles? After all, he was home during the day. Why didn't he tell me what testicles were for and what it meant to be a man with the power to create life? Why didn't he tell me about masturbation so I wouldn't have had to go through years thinking I was doing a terrible thing to myself? Why didn't he tell about his infidelities and how they occurred so that when I was tempted in my own marriage, I would have an understanding of how men and women related or didn't relate? Why didn't he protect me?

My mother's tirade against my writing to my father scared me. Never before had I confronted non-existence. She meant every word. If I had anything to do with my father, I was no longer her son. I couldn't win. One way or another I would lose a parent. As I wrestled with this losing proposition, I realized that my father never gave me anything to convince me that I should go to his side. For me, at the age of twenty, my father was mostly a non-entity. My only attraction to him was my need to have a father.

I remember on my tenth birthday, my parents took me to dinner at the Roosevelt Grill in New York City. I asked my father if I could have my picture taken with Lombardo. In those days, attractive young women dressed as if they were ballerinas walked through the Grill with a reporter's style camera and a bag of flash bulbs to take pictures of the patrons so they could have a memory of their evening out. During an intermission, my father arranged for one of the young women to come to Guy's table and take my picture with him. When I got to the table Guy stood up, shook my hand, and with a big grin said, "Happy Birthday, Walter." He asked me how I was and how I was doing in school. I always liked Guy, or Mr. Lombardo, as I called him. Every time he saw me, he stopped and chatted with me for several minutes. His wife, Lillibel, would have me sit next to her when we were at the East Point House, the restaurant Lombardo owned near

Jones Beach, New York, and where he kept his speedboat, Tempo VI. I sat down next to Lombardo with my shoulder resting next to his chest and my hands folded in my lap. He had his arm around my chair and a big smile on his face. My father was in the picture, too. He was about eighteen inches from me, squatting down with his hand on the back of my chair, and his mouth opened as if he was in the beginning of a smile. When I showed the picture to a friend of mine about ten years ago, he said, "You know, Walter, if I didn't know any better, I would've thought Lombardo was your father—your father looks uncomfortable, he looks so distant."

The fear of losing my mother's love led me to suspend contact with my father. If I lost my mother, I was afraid I would cease to exist. She was my grounding in the world—I was the fruit of her womb. She also gave me room and board, and she was always at those important events of my life. Regardless of my feelings about my mother, she was the only stability I had in the world. To ignore her warning about having a relationship with my father would be disastrous. I would not only be going to an unknown relationship with my father, but I would also be severing all connections to the only stability I knew. It was hard enough to feel alone the world, but to sever all contacts with the world was jumping into a void I could not bear to imagine. All through college and seminary, I had minimal contact with my father. Yet, I thought about him constantly. There was not a birthday or Christmas that went by without a card and money from him and a request (a plea?) for me to write.

I graduated from San Francisco Theological Seminary in June 1967. I sent my father an announcement of my graduation. I wasn't going to let this moment pass without his knowing it regardless of what my mother said. My mother was present for the ceremony, and afterwards I was talking with a few of my friends when a Western Union messenger delivered a telegram to me. It was from my father. It read, "Good luck and congratulations on your graduation. Received your letter and very nice picture. Wish you the best of everything for your future. Let me know where I can write you before you leave for Scotland. Love, Dad." That August I traveled to Glasgow, Scotland, where I would be for the next year as the Assistant Minister of the Croftfoot Parish Church in Croftfoot, a suburb of Glasgow. When I arrived back in August of 1968, I visited some relatives and friends of my parents. I also called my father.

"Hi, Dad."

"Walter, I'm so glad to hear you. I've missed you."

"I've missed you too, Dad. I don't want us to be separated."

"I need you, son."

That phone call made me realize how much I needed my father and how much he needed me. I determined that I would have to face the fear of life without my mother. I loved her, but I, also, realized that her demands were unhealthy. If I did what she wanted, I would cease to be the person God wanted me to be. I couldn't let another human being determine who I should or should not love. That was only for God to decide, and as far as I could tell, God never stops loving anyone. As important as my mother's love was to me, what was more important was for me to do God's will. For my own sake, for the sake of my faith, and for the sake of my father, I realized that I would have to come to terms with the fact that I might have to live the rest of my life without my mother's love.

~

My wife and I were married in 1970 when I was twenty-eight and she twenty-one. Two years later we traveled to the Pocono Mountains in Pennsylvania where my father and step-mother lived. When he saw our car pull up in the dirt driveway of his dark brown wooden A-frame cabin, he ran out to the car. I hardly got the door open before his arms enveloped me. We hugged and cried, both realizing it had been ten years since we had seen each other. The next morning my father and I took a long walk together in the woods.

"Walter, you need to know my side of the story. You've only got their (meaning my mother and grandmother) side of the story. I wasn't perfect, but I had a hellava battle to fight with those two. Don't you think I know what your grandmother told your mother about me when she came home from work? How I was a lazy, drunken bum. I couldn't satisfy that woman. She complained that I didn't get what she wanted from the grocery store, but then she didn't tell me all she wanted."

"I know, Dad. I remember the times when she complained about not going out to eat and then when we made plans, she said she felt sick and couldn't go."

"I couldn't understand your mother, either. I tried to tell her how much I loved her. I would put my arms around her and want to kiss her, but she would say, "Get away from me, you old fart." Betty (my stepmother) and I were at a horse ranch. We saw a male horse mount a female. Just as he was about to penetrate her, she would run out from under him. This happened several times until the male gave up. That's the way your mother was with me. That's the way she was with other men, too. She'd led them on and then she'd run out from under them. When we bought the house in the valley (San Fernando Valley, California), I told her the only way we could afford the house was to have a second mortgage. The owner was willing to loan us the money and we would pay monthly interest for five years and then pay the principle in full. She said she understood, but when it came time to pay the principle, she accused me of duping her. She told me that I never told her what would happen, for if I did, she would never have agreed to it. That year before we finally broke up, I sent her $900.00 a month. I lived on hardly anything that year. I sent it all to her. I was hoping that we could save up to remodel the house, only to find out when I got out to California that she didn't have a penny of it, and she didn't know where it went. Can you see my side of the story?"

"What I want to know, Dad, is why didn't you leave sooner?"

We were silent for a while and listened to the leaves and the branches crackling under our feet. I knew I had to confront my father with my feelings but I was anxious about doing so. He was smaller than I was, but he was my father and he had the authority of that role. Also, the years of silence never allowed me the opportunity to test him and find out what I could and couldn't say. I didn't know how he would react, and I feared I might lose him. I also knew that my mother would know of my being with my father. My father's cousin, Anna, who knew I was visiting him and who didn't approve of my father's infidelity, reported every move he made to my mother. So with this visit, I knew that I had taken the road less traveled; I had chosen of my own free will to risk being disowned by my mother. As the years went by, I would not be disappointed. If my father rejected me, however, I would lose them both. But I knew I couldn't leave my father without confronting him about the emptiness he bequeathed to me.

"Dad," I said, "I know you and Mom had problems. That's not where I am right now. Growing up I needed a father and you weren't there. I know Mom was a bitch, because I know what she did to me and you weren't there to protect me when she was putting her hands up my pants in front of other women. You never cared about anything I did for you. That workbench I had made for you, you never said it was nice or thanked me for it.

The only thing you could say was that it might be too heavy to hang in the garage. You wouldn't even take it with us when we moved to California; 'it would add too much to the moving cost,' you said. How the hell do you think that made me feel? You wouldn't even come to my wedding. I took extra pains to arrange a truce between you and Mom because I wanted you both there. Do you realize the risk I took for you? Mom told me if I had any contact with you, I was no longer her son. Damn it Dad, I needed you both and you both screwed me. You left me to raise myself because you two were too busy worrying about your own problems. There are times when I wished you never had me."

My father was silent. We stopped walking. He turned to me and in a soft voice he said, "I know, Walter. I've been a lousy father to you. I don't deserve your love or forgiveness and I will not ask for them. You have every right to feel the way you do. I failed you as a father. I'm sorry."

Tears welled up in my eyes. It was the first time anyone ever apologized to me. I hugged him. We both started to cry. That was all I needed to hear him say. In those few words, he released my anger by accepting it. We would still have our difficulties in the years to come, but I knew that my father loved me and I loved him. My father who had abandoned me was now reclaiming me as his son. In the coming years, I would have similar conversations with God. I like to think that my courage to confront my earthly father gave me the courage to confront my heavenly father whom I, also, felt had abandoned me.

> Jesus said, "But if any one strikes you on the right cheek, turn to him the other also; and if any one would sue you and take your coat, let him have your cloak as well; and if any one forces you to go one mile, go with him two miles.[1]

This above passage is often misinterpreted to mean that if someone hits you should let that person continue to hit you even if it results in your death. That's not what Jesus is getting at. We are not to be punching bags for people who may hate us. What I think Jesus is saying is that if someone is angry enough to strike us or sue us, then maybe we have done something to elicit that behavior. No one is without fault, and in any conflicted situation there's enough blame to go around. By turning the other cheek, we become vulnerable to the other person. We open ourselves up to hearing what the other has against us. We are saying, "My friend, I must have

---

1. Matt 5:39–41.

done something wrong to make you want to strike me or sue me. Please tell me what it is so that we can heal the rift between us." That's what my father did to me. He turned the other cheek. He could have reacted defensively and given me all kinds of excuses for not doing what he should have done. Instead, he accepted his responsibility and his guilt and by doing so, he made it possible for me to forgive him. All I wanted at this point of my life was for someone to admit that my family had treated me shabbily. I wanted someone to acknowledge the pain I was feeling and that it wasn't the result of what I did.

This is what Jesus did on the cross. The religious leaders of his day were angry because he did not lead an uprising against the hated Roman Empire. The Romans hated him because he claimed there was a God other than Caesar, and they crucified him for treason. He took all the anger and the pain of the people on himself, and because he didn't return it, it stopped. The greatest obstacle to being a Christian is to accept that it is through suffering, and not returning evil for evil, that we end suffering. We don't like to suffer. I'm sure that for my father to hear those words come from my mouth was painful for him. I was afraid that I could lose him at that moment, but he must have been afraid that he might lose me, too.

Forgiveness is often a simple thing to do, especially when the offender recognizes his or her fault and takes responsibility, when the offender turns the other cheek. This did not end the problems between my father and me, for in coming years we would have some difficult conversations. However, my father always kept in touch, calling on the phone, visiting his grandchildren, and I reciprocated. The lines of communication stayed opened; he wanted me as his son, and I wanted him as my father.

8

I Give Up, God: Forgiving My Mother

Then Peter came and said to him, "Lord, if another member of the church sins against me, how often should I forgive? As many as seven times?" Jesus said to him, "Not seven times, but, I tell you, seventy times seven.

MATT 18: 21-22

Jesus looked at them and said, "For mortals it is impossible, but not for God; for God all things are possible."

MARK 10:27

FORGIVING MY MOTHER WAS not as easy as forgiving my father. My father admitted that he failed me, and in the process, he honored me; he told me I was a valid individual and my cause was just. My mother, on the other hand, was of the opinion that she did nothing wrong and whatever problems I had with her, were of my own making and my desire to hurt her. She refused to talk to me about the pain in our relationship, maintaining that she was a good mother, and that I was an ingrate for not recognizing how blessed I was to have a mother like her.

In June 2000, I received a call from Eastern New Mexico Medical Center in Roswell saying that my mother was in the hospital with a fractured hip and bleeding from the rectum. The hospital told me that she couldn't go back to her home and would be sent to a nursing home once they pinned her hip and performed a colonoscopy, which showed a cancerous tumor.

My mother had lived in Roswell with her mother and brother since 1971 when they moved there from Hollywood, California. My parents had been divorced for ten years. A friend of hers had told her that the

United States government was auctioning homes that were originally used to house military personnel and their families who were stationed at the Walker Air Force Base. The base was closed on order of President Lyndon Johnson in 1967. Some saw the closing as further evidence that the government wanted to stop all inquiries into the supposed crash of a UFO in 1947. The base is now used as a flight training school for major airlines and as a municipal airport. It has a two-mile, six-foot thick concrete runway. My mother took a trip to Roswell, put a bid on a home, which was accepted, and informed her mother and brother they were moving.

My mother bought a single story, rectangular, green stucco, ranch style, 900 square foot house with an attached carport on Greenbrier. Upon entering the front door, you were immediately in the small, square living room with a brown, red, and gold shag rug, beige stucco walls, and two half-windows facing the street. If you came in too fast, you might run into the TV console, which was an old floor model Zenith that took up most of the left wall. Immediately behind the living room was the kitchen, and a hallway from the living room led to the bathroom, and three bedrooms. The back yard was deep and surrounded by a solid wood picket fence that allowed for privacy. A large pear tree in the middle of the yard demanded most of the moisture, which in this arid climate made growing grass unthinkable. The yard was mostly dirt and weeds.

By the time I got out to New Mexico, two weeks later, my mother was in the Mission Arch Care Center, a single story, beige stucco, Spanish style building. Lena, her next-door neighbor, told me she was found unconscious by some of the neighborhood children who came to see her and saw her lying on the floor through the living room window.

The house was filthy and smelled of dog and cat feces and urine. I had to wear a surgical mask to go into the house to try to cut down on the odor. "The city came and took the animals away," Lena told me. I was glad about that since I would not have known what to do with them. Her situation must have deteriorated rapidly since I was out to see her just three years before, when the house was clean and she seemed to be getting along well for her eighty-seven years. Ten years earlier, I had asked her to come to live with me in Virginia. She refused saying she wouldn't do that to me. Part of me was appreciative because I saw the havoc her mother had caused in our family as I was growing up. But I was hoping that living together in the last few years of her life might bring some reconciliation and closure, and it would also give my sons a chance to know their grandmother.

On the other hand, her refusal felt like a rejection of me. While she was excited at the news of the birth of her grandsons, the excitement seemed to dissipate as they grew. Their birthday cards always arrived three to five weeks late, and I often had to call her and tell her she missed their birthdays. She was unable to understand that my salary just didn't allow us to spend close to two thousand dollars on travel to New Mexico when she insisted that I had the obligation to bring my family to visit her because she had to take care of her mother and brother and she couldn't possibly come to visit us. Yet, she and her brother went to visit my father's cousin, Anna, in Pennsylvania and never told me that they were going nor did they call us when they were there. We only lived a few hundred miles away, at the time, and could have easily gone up to see her. I got the distinct impression that she was punishing me for having a relationship with my father.

I went to see her at the Mission Arch Care Center. I stopped at the nurses' station located at the intersection of two hallways running perpendicular to each other and introduced myself. They told me my mother was doing as well as could be expected given what she had been through. Her hip no longer gave her pain but she was losing blood slowly. She was in the skilled care unit, which meant she was getting round-the-clock monitoring.

I had no idea what to expect from my mother when I first saw her, but the nurse gave me a hint when she told me that my mother was refusing to let her roommate into the room. I went to my mother's room and found her parked in her wheelchair in the doorway.

"What's the matter, Mom?"

"She hasn't paid me my rent and I'm not going to let her back in this room."

I had been to a conference the year before on dementia. The leader told us that when you cannot reason with a demented person, you might have to resort to creative lying. This was one of those times.

"Yes, she did, Mom. In fact, I just came from the bank where I deposited her check in your account."

"Oh, okay, Walt." Then she let her roommate back in the room and gave me a hug and a kiss.

While this story is humorous, it's also sad. I was standing before a woman whom I recognized and knew for sixty years. The voice was the same; she called everyone "honey" or "toots" as she had throughout her life. Her smile, her gestures, her blue sparkling eyes were all there. In her old age, she was still beautiful and her breasts had mostly maintained their shape. The nurses wanted to know if I had a picture of her when she was a young woman; they thought she must have been a real beauty for her to look as beautiful as she did now. I gave them a picture of her in her early twenties, which they put up on the wall by her bed. I felt sorry for myself more than I did for her. She didn't know any better. She had pleaded with me many times during her life not to put her into a nursing home. When she got to the nursing home, she had no understanding of where she was; she had even forgotten that she had cats and dogs at home. The sadness for me was knowing that I would never be able to be reconciled to her or her to me in this life. How do you forgive a person with whom you cannot reconcile; with whom there is no possibility of reconciliation? How do you find peace in your life when the source of that peace is gone? How do you live the rest of your life knowing that when your mother dies you will not grieve for her passing?

～

"What do you think your mother's life was like as a child?" my counselor, Dr. Beata Cronin, a clinical psychologist asked. I didn't want to hear that question although I knew it was coming since she had been leading up to it in our sessions over the past several weeks with allusions to the fact that my mother could have had a painful childhood. I had started seeing Dr. Cronin several months after I came back from my visit to New Mexico. I hated the question. I didn't want to think about my mother's childhood. The sexual, emotional, and verbal abuse I received from her had led me to know that I was correct in believing that she was not entitled to any consideration about her childhood or any empathy on my part. The only constant in my life had been emotional pain, which coalesced with a vengeance in the 1990s. Reconciliation with my mother was becoming impossible. I identified myself as a victim and that title hung on my shoulders like a thousand pound ball and chain that couldn't be removed. The muscles in my body were always tight, and I ached with every move I made. I couldn't get excited about anything and I went about my work with a malaise that was suffocating. The only redeeming part of my life was that I managed, somehow, to carry on with my work and responsibilities despite it all.

My consumption of wine increased during this time. In the Bible, wine is the symbol of the presence of God, and I rationalized my drinking by thinking that the more wine I drank, the more of God I would have available to me have since I felt I had nothing else. I realized something was terribly wrong when one night I went downstairs, sat at my desk, put my head into my arms, and cried. My wife came down, put her hand on my shoulder, and asked what she could do for me. I am sure my answer shocked her because it shocked me. I said, "I want to go home." I meant I wanted to die. I was tired of all the pain, of all the doubts, of all the questions; I was worn out hoping I could find love from my mother. How dare my counselor, Dr. Cronin, ask me that question? I came to her because I was looking for comfort and solace from a woman, and all she could do was ask me to consider the life of a woman who was destroying me.

However, I always had the ability to listen to my doctors and counselors even when they told me things I didn't like to hear. I gave them the benefit of the doubt because I reasoned they were the authority in their field, just as I was in mine. I also remembered what a counselor had said to me thirty years ago: "Your mother gave you many problems, but now they are yours and you have to deal with them responsibly." In addition, my years of psychotherapy taught me to recognize when I was in trouble and needed to seek help. After that night with my wife, and before I met Dr. Cronin, I found a psychiatrist who helped me with my drinking. He told me that he didn't think I was an alcoholic, but reacting more to my present circumstances. He taught me how to think rationally about the effects of alcohol on my body, my life, and my family. However, he got my attention when he told me that the alcohol intensified my depression the night I wanted to die by at least ten-fold. That if I had taken my life it would have been because of a self-induced depression that appeared to be greater than what it was in reality. It scared me to realize that I could have ended it all for something that was manageable. He put me on five milligrams of Prozac once a day. The depression lifted, and I greatly reduced my consumption of alcohol.

When Dr. Cronin asked her question, part of me wanted to lash out in anger and tell her I wasn't going to think about what my mother's life was like when she was a child. But I didn't. I was in too much pain, and nothing relieved it. Why not face the unthinkable, and prepare myself to admit that my mother may have had a more painful childhood than she gave to me, and that we might be more alike than different, and that the only way to get relief was to forgive her?

I also had to forgive her because my Lord and Savior Jesus Christ told us to forgive one another, and I, a Presbyterian minister, could hardly ignore that command. Also, how could I preach on forgiveness and not be able to do it myself? Dr. Cronin's question put me on the path of healing, the path I needed to take, but I did not take it willingly or joyfully and I knew there were many perils ahead. I resisted it until the pain of not forgiving her was far greater than the pain I would endure by going through the process of forgiveness.

I was afraid to forgive my mother. Forgiveness meant that I would have let her go and give up all hope for any kind of reconciliation even though I knew reconciliation was out of the question at this point. I wanted to be angry with my mother; it was the only way to keep her indebted to me for her actions. Forgiveness would release her from her responsibility. I would be letting her go free as if I was saying, "Oh, it doesn't matter." Just as I needed my father to honor and respect my personhood by admitting to his mistakes, I needed my mother to grant me the same honor and respect.

My fear wasn't just about my releasing my mother from her responsibilities. I also feared that if I let my mother go, I would cease to exist. Who would I be without my mother? She was the ground of my being, the one who gave me life. In spite of whatever she did, she was still my mother, I loved her, and I needed her. If I gave up my claim to the ground of my being, would I be giving up my own life? I wasn't so much afraid of dying physically, although that thought crossed my mind, as becoming a nonperson. I could see myself walking around as an empty container—not able to love or care about anything.

Sixteen years earlier, I was in counseling. My therapist, a Baptist pastor, Howard Doerle, was slowly but steadily getting me to admit that I had been abused. I didn't want to admit I was abused; it was embarrassing to admit to another person that someone had hurt me. It made me feel vulnerable and weak. It also called into question my integrity. Was I abused because I was a bad child? Was I the one to blame and not my parents?

The day I finally admitted to the abuse, Doerle asked me to draw a word picture describing my sense of hopelessness. I said, "I am inside a well, I can't see the bottom, it's dark. I have one hand on the top rim, the other has just fallen off, and I'm afraid I am going to fall and there will be nothing to catch me; I will just keep falling into the darkness for all eternity." Doerle said, "As you hold on to the well, know that I'm holding on to you and I will not let you fall." I left my counselor's office and drove the forty-five minute trip home. The sun, looking like a big orange ball, was setting behind me on this warm day as I drove through the row of trees that embraced the sides of Interstate 40 from Morganton to Statesville, North Carolina. As I looked in my rear view mirror as the sun continued its descent, I wondered if I would see it rise in the morning. I kept thinking about turning my car into the on coming traffic and ending it all. I was no good to anyone; my family would be better off without me—this hunk of painful clay. When I got home, I don't remember seeing or talking to my wife or children. Maybe they weren't home; maybe they were and I was too preoccupied to let anyone in my life. I went into the bathroom, closed the door, put the lid down on the toilet, sat down, and cried. I said, "God, I don't know if you exist or not, but if you do, you better do something fast because I don't believe anymore."

I never attempted to take my life. Even when I was thinking of turning my car into oncoming traffic, my hands stayed steady on the wheel. I like to think that was God keeping me alive long enough to be able to believe again. I kept my appointments with Doerle faithfully, and over the months, he helped me to see that I was not the cause of the abuse I received. He told me that when we are children we just assume that we are omnipotent and are the cause of things that happen to us. When we become adults, we know different, but those childhood ideas stay with us. He helped me to see my father's neglect of me was the result of what his parents did to him. "Be grateful that he didn't beat you." Slowly, I began to forgive myself for something I never did.

Howard also got me in touch with my inner child, the hurt little boy inside me.

"I bet there's a neat little boy inside you. Have you ever talked to him?" he said.

"No, how can I, I'm no longer a child."

"But you can. Imagine yourself as a child. What age would you be?"

"I guess I would be eight years old," I said.

"Good, now I want you to remember what you looked like at eight. Now just imagine that little boy is sitting next to you. What would you say to him?"

"I would tell him that I was sorry he had such a lousy life, that I blamed him for my problems, and that I would like to get to know him," I said.

"Good. Your homework is to take walks with your little child and listen to what he has to say."

I did as Doerle said. As my child and I walked and talked, we told each other what our life was like. He told me he had a rough time, but he sure did like what I had become; he was proud of me. One day, I looked at him and he at me:

"I love you," I said.

"I love you, too."

As we continued in therapy, Doerle suggested that I do something nice for myself every day. It didn't have to cost money, but it did have to be something that I would enjoy. At first, I objected.

"Howard, it sounds like you want me to put my needs ahead of others. Wouldn't that be selfish?"

"The only way you will be healed is to start caring for yourself. Jesus often went off by himself to get away from the madding crowd, if I can borrow the title of a book."

"Yes, but when they came after him, he met their needs."

"But he still went off by himself; he knew he needed time to be renewed. He could meet the needs of the people who followed him because he took time to be with his God and nurtured himself."

"What about Jesus' coming to be a servant and not to be served?"

Howard said, "Well, what about Jesus saying that you should love your neighbor as YOURSELF? We often hear only 'love your neighbor.' We very seldom hear 'love yourself.' I tell you the only way you are going to get out from under your mother's spell, Walter, and the only way you are going to be healed is to start giving yourself the nurturing your mother never gave you."

I began seeing what Howard was saying lived out in real life. I remembered reading an interview with the pianist, Arthur Rubenstein. He was asked whom he played for in his concerts. His answer shocked the interviewer. He said he played for himself. When the interviewer challenged him on not caring for his audience, he said that if he didn't play to satisfy himself, he wouldn't satisfy anyone else, either. On an airplane, the flight attendant tells passengers with small children that if the oxygen masks drop down they are to put the mask on themselves first and then the child.

The point is that if you didn't take care of yourself first, you would be of no use to the child if you lost consciousness.

It was hard for me, at first, to do something nice for myself. The first time I did something nice for me was when I masturbated, but then I was filled with guilt. Now Howard was asking me to move beyond that and see a completely new world where I could satisfy myself in deeper and more significant ways.

I always wanted to be in a play and our neighbor, Julie Holland, at the time was casting for the play *1776* to be performed by the Community Theater in Statesville, North Carolina in 1987. They needed someone to play the Reverend Jonathan Witherspoon, a Presbyterian and the only minister to sign the declaration of Independence. I auditioned and got the part. It was a small part, but the cast, some of which were "old hands" at acting, received me warmly. I noticed during rehearsals that many of the actors ceased being who they were in real life and took on the personality of the character they were playing. I had a difficult time doing that until the night of our first performance.

It was near the end of the play. The Continental Congress had gathered in Philadelphia. The old brown floor of the stage theater creaked under our weight as we shifted back and forth on our old wooden chairs and fidgeted with our quill pens. The theater was warm and humid, and we sweated under our costumes made from heavy drapery material and the black, heavy meshed panty hose we had to wear. I often wondered if we were sweating more from heat or from fear. George Washington had written the Continental Congress that things were going badly and he prayed for the strength from the almighty. During the reading of Washington's letter, fear overcame me for what the British might do to our cause, and I had the feeling that all we worked for could be lost. I feared for my life. I could see myself being hanged by the hated British, and I wondered if what I did was what God wanted me to do. Who can tell what God wants? I thought. I felt alone, as I am sure my brothers in the Continental Congress felt. Did we make some drastic mistake? Were we going to be the fools of history? Of course, at this point I had become the Reverend Jonathan Witherspoon. I was one with my comrades in our quest for independence.

The struggle of the Continental Congress for independence was not unlike my own. I needed to be independent of my mother as much as my ancestors needed to be independent of King George. Declaring independence was scary, however. I was making decisions with no assurance of the outcome. I felt alone as much as my comrades in Congress, realizing I was in no less of a fight for my life than those who fought for the independence of our country. My argument with Doerle over Biblical issues concerning self-care was only a smoke screen hiding my fear that if Doerle was right, I would become independent enough to give up my mother or at least admit that our relationship was based only on biology. A decision I saw, at that time, as both physically and spiritually deadly.

As time went on, it became easier for me to do nice things for myself. I began praying and meditating for up to an hour a day, I took walks, often with my little child, I stopped watching television and started reading books, and I lost forty pounds and made myself a good breakfast every morning. I began to see that I didn't get as upset with my sons as I once did. I started to let my wife be herself and enjoyed what she could bring to our family. Things that normally bothered me were no longer important. This wasn't instantaneous, however. It took years to develop and in many ways, it is still developing. A few years ago, I heard Marian Woodman, a Jungian analyst, at the International Conference of the Association for Psychological Type say that if you have a negative mother image, which is the most difficult image to overcome, you need to be into good self-care.

As I struggled with the fear of forgiving my mother, I knew I had been through this valley of the shadow of death before.[1] It was still frightening, however. This time I did believe in God even though I still harbored doubts about God's ability to help, and I knew I would not give up that belief and that was comforting. I was also into good self-care. I had come to the point where I knew that doing the right thing, whether or not the other person appreciated it, was the best thing for me to do. It's like doing God's will. People may hate you or even praise you for doing it, but the one who benefits the most is you. I began to realize that I needed to forgive my mother not because she deserved it, but because it would make me a better person; it would make me more into the person God wanted me to be. That's why we need to go through the struggle to forgive. If the other person benefits then that is added satisfaction. Often, however, the other person doesn't know they are forgiven or even care.

My relationship with God over the next several months was not pleasant. I was furious because I had to take my time and energy to for-

1. Ps 23.

give a person who didn't deserve it. It was stopping me from doing things I wanted to do, like write this book. It was interfering with my life; there was more to life than having to forgive a woman who would not know if she was forgiven and would not care. What good was this stupid command to forgive when I would never enjoy the love that should exist between a mother and a son? I issued a challenge, and said to God: "If you want me to forgive then you will have to give me the power to forgive, because I cannot and will not do it."

Dr. Cronin's question haunted me. As I said, I had no desire to think of my mother's life as she was growing up. However, she had given me hints all through her life that created in me suspicions of her relationship with her father.

In 1997, I was visiting my mother in Roswell, New Mexico. We were sitting in her small living room. Her old Airdale wandered back and forth between the living room and one of the bedrooms obviously nervous and uncomfortable.

"She does that all the time," my mother said.

"She needs to be put to sleep," I said.

"I know, but I can't bring myself to do that."

My mother sat at the end of the sofa she bought when I was a child. I sat in the blue armchair that was my grandmother's but now it was gold after its third reupholstering. If you drew a line from me to the corner of the room then over to my mother and back to me we would have formed an equilateral triangle. We were talking about the family. I asked her if I could record our conversation. She was in her late eighties and I knew I didn't have much more time to collect family stories.

"Promise me you won't tell anyone," my mother said.

"Promise you I won't tell anybody what?" I said.

"What I am going to tell you," she said.

"What are you going to tell me?"

"I can't tell you unless you promise me you won't tell anyone," she said.

This is juicy, I thought. She wants to tell me one of the great family secrets. I want to hear it. But I'm also a writer. If it's juicy, how can I stop from writing it? So I lied.

"I promise," I said.

That was the way it was with my mother. It never mattered if you carried out your promise; what was important was that you promised.

"Papa was a wonderful man. He was in the Navy, you know?"

"Yes, I know," I said. Ever since I was a babe, I heard that Grandpa served in the Spanish American War and World War I.

"Papa took me to the shipyards in Brooklyn one night for dinner on board ship. He bought me a new dress, white gloves, and a necklace. My mother didn't want to go, so he took me," my mother said. "We were served fried chicken. I was trying to eat it with my knife and fork and the Captain of the ship leaned over and said to me: 'Just pick it up in your hands, missy.' He was such a nice man. Then my father and I would walk home, hand-in-hand, laughing."

"What is it you don't want me to tell?" I said.

"Just a second, I'm getting to that part."

"Your grandfather knew everyone. He loved the Fire Department. He took care of the horses. He brushed them down everyday, fed them, and worked with the Dalmatian during a fire to help quiet the horses. He was always bringing a stray animal home to feed and nurse back to health. He wasn't afraid of anything," my mother said. "When he died he left me all of his money, fifteen hundred dollars."

"Nothing to Granny?" I said.

"Nothing, not even to my brother, Bob. He didn't like Bob's running around with all those floozy women and drinking his money away."

My mother's other two brothers were her mother's by a previous marriage so they didn't figure into Grandpa's formula for dividing his estate. For the first time in my life, I had empathy for my uncle. From experiences with my own father, I could imagine the pain my uncle felt at being rejected by his. No wonder he became an alcoholic.

"Mom, you still haven't told me what you don't want me to tell," I said. I was beginning to wonder if she doubted my promise. The tape recorder was running but I think she had forgotten about that.

"Papa also liked parties and from Thanksgiving to New Year's Day we had one party after another at the house. We always had plenty of liquor and this was Prohibition days," she said.

"Where did you get it?"

"Twice a year, Papa would put on his dress fireman's uniform and take a car to Montauk Point. Someone gave him the car because we didn't own one," she said.

Montauk Point was at the end of Long Island, New York. It was almost deserted except for a lighthouse that guided the ships coming into the New York harbor or going farther south. It was over a hundred miles from Brooklyn.

"He'd leave early in the afternoon and wouldn't get back for two days. I asked him what he was doing. He only told me he went to Montauk Point," she said. I have the feeling he was 'bootlegging' for Joe Kennedy."

"What! You mean our family has ties to the Kennedy's?" I said. "If I ever meet Teddy Kennedy, I'll remind him that my grandfather helped his father get rich."

"Oh, he never knew Kennedy, but it was known in those days that Joe Kennedy was smuggling liquor into the States. The ships would anchor off of Montauk Point and send the liquor to the beach on their life boats where it would be picked up and taken into the city," she said.

"And Grandpa was one of the runners?"

"It would make sense. The police wouldn't stop someone in a fireman's uniform; they would think he was on official business. Now, I don't have any proof of this. But Papa's going to Montauk Point and the fact that we had so much liquor in the house that he never paid for made me suspicious."

"That's a neat story," I said.

"But you have to promise me not to tell anyone. I would be very embarrassed," she said.

"I promise," I said. "You really loved your father, didn't you? You know Mom, in all the years, I never heard you say one negative thing about him. I wonder if there was anything he did that hurt you?"

"Now why do you have to think of things such as that?"

I knew I'd hit a sore spot, but I remained quiet.

"My father never told me he loved me, but I knew he loved me. He was always buying me things and making sure that I had enough money. I remember one night when I was about ten. I heard him and my mother arguing. I got out of bed and sat on the top landing of the stairs. I could see him choking my mother. He must have heard me, because he stopped."

"Didn't that frighten you?"

"Not really. I knew they didn't get along. He loved me and would take me places and buy things for me, but he wouldn't take my mother any place. Then again she wouldn't go with him."

I was amazed my mother was not upset about seeing her father choke her mother. I wondered if secretly she wanted her mother out of the way much like the proverbial Oedipal boy who wants to kill his father so he can marry his mother. As a counselor, I become suspicious of people who present a parent or spouse in glowing terms and never say anything bad about them. It says to me that they are denying some negative and shameful behaviors. No one is a perfect parent or spouse. Even when a parent or spouse dies, we grieve, but there are also things we will not miss about them. Families often keep secrets and this is one way to do it. In addition, my mother was always anxious and easily startled. That is often a sign of abuse. The description of my grandfather taking my mother to social events, buying her new clothes for the event, giving her money, and walking home hand-in-hand describes the relationship of lovers more than father and daughter. While I have no concrete evidence, I cannot help but think that given my mother's beauty he sexually molested her and then paid her off.

At the same time Dr. Cronin asked me the question, I was taking an online writing class on creating dynamic characters. At this point, I was into fiction writing, and I thought the best way to get rid of Dr. Cronin's question was to write a story about a young girl who was abused by her father. I based the story on my eighth grade art teacher because she suffered so much in her conflict with the Communists. I put her in the context of being with her father before WWII and gave her the name of Victoria. However, the story was meant to be about my mother. This is what I wrote.

"Victoria, I'm ready to leave for the park."

"Daddy, I don't want to go."

"Why, you've always liked the park?"

"I do, but Mommy's sick."

"Mommy is no more sick than she's ever been."

"But the doctor has been here three times this week."

"You have nothing to worry about."

Victoria didn't believe her daddy. When the doctor came, he and Frederic went into Gisele's room and closed the door. Victoria listened at the keyhole. It was hard to understand their muffled voices, but one time she heard the doctor say, "We need to get her undressed." A few minutes later she heard her mother groaning and pleading, "Please stop."

"Now, let's go to the park and draw the blooming tulips," her father said as he clasped his daughter's hand and they began their walk to the park.

"How did Mommy get sick, Daddy?"

"She got sick just after you were born. Some women become sad after they have a child. The doctor calls it 'the blues'. Most of the time they get better, but your Mommy didn't."

"Then I made Mommy sick?"

"That's not true," he said in a halfhearted tone, relieved that Victoria thought it was her fault. Maybe he could begin to forget what really happened. Gisele 'got the blues' shortly after she found out she was pregnant. She didn't want a child but her husband did. They fought about it. One night, in his fury he raped her. "How dare you refuse me," he remembered saying to her as he thrust himself inside of her. Afterward, he had to take her to the doctor—she required five stitches.

"What will happen if Mommy dies?"

"Mommy isn't going to die," he said, irritated at his daughter's questions.

"Yes, she is, and I will be left alone."

"No, you will not, you will always have me. Now shut up."

"I wish I was never born," Victoria sobbed.

Frederic stopped to wipe away her tears. He told her he was sorry for yelling at her. He felt powerless to help his daughter.

"Oh, look at the beautiful flowers in the park. We can draw them, and you can take your drawing home for Mommy. That will make her feel better."

He took Victoria by the hand and they ran the last hundred feet to the park. They spread the blanket on the grass and Victoria opened the picnic basket. On the top of their lunch was a brightly wrapped large, rectangular box.

"What's this, Daddy?"

"Open it, it's for you."

"A new box of chalk! Oh, thank you, Daddy." She lunged at him and gave him a hug.

After lunch, they began looking at the tulips they wanted to sketch. He helped her to understand that when you look at an object what you see is not so much the object but light waves of different lengths. Depending on the length of the wave the object appears lighter or darker thus giving it shape and depth.

"Look at this yellow tulip," Frederic said. "You see the sun is creating a shadow inside the flower. It doesn't change the color of the flower but the shadow makes it darker. So you want to use a darker chalk to create the shadow effect and show that you are looking into the flower." He guided her hand as Victoria captured the tulip on her sketchpad.

"Excellent. You're going to make Mommy feel so much better."

Victoria was proud of her drawing. She got up and began to run. "Catch me if you can," she yelled to her father. Frederic chased after his daughter. She ran toward the hill. When he caught her, they fell to the ground and rolled down the hill laughing, coming to rest behind some bushes. Victoria was on her back. Frederic was lying on his side with one arm around her back and another on her chest just under her undeveloped breast.

"I love you, Daddy." She threw her arms around his neck to hug him. As her face started to move to the side of his, he intercepted it and greeted her lips with his opened lips. Victoria pulled away from his face as best as she could.

"Daddy, I feel funny."

"It's okay, honey."

Victoria lay back on the grass. She was frightened. Her father never did anything like this to her before.

"Daddy, can we go home now?...Mommy needs us...please."

As I typed the last quotation mark, I broke down in tears. I have no way of knowing if this is what happened to my mother, but I don't think it is far from the truth. Dr. Cronin was right, my mother suffered greatly as a child. Her father made her his little wife just as she made me her little man. The hurt little boy in me could identify with the hurt little girl in my mother. I realized that like my father, my mother's life was probably more painful than my own, and while that did not excuse her for what she did, I came to realize that she, like my father, did the best she could for me with what little she had been given. I was more like her than different from her because we were hurt little children walking on this earth together. It was at that point that I felt the pain, the anger, and the stress over not being able to forgive her melt away. My shoulders were no longer tight and heavy, and I no longer considered myself a victim. The curse had been lifted. I began to live more fully in the joy and the grace of God, and I realized that I had indeed forgiven my mother all because I had seen a vision of her own unbridled suffering.

It has been six years since I wrote that story. Only recently have I come across notes that I made of my visit with my mother in 1994, which I had forgotten. The notes tell another story. My mother and I were listening to Oprah Winfrey one afternoon when Oprah said that her father was her best friend.

"I wish I could say that about my father," my mother said.

"What do you mean, Mom? All my life, you have only talked in loving terms about him and what a great man he was. How he took you to places and bought things for you and how you loved being with him."

"I know. But in all those times he never touched me, hugged me, or kissed me, and he never said he loved me. My mother didn't either. I said to my mother when I was a girl that I thought that Papa didn't love me. She said, 'what do you mean, you're his favorite.' But he never told me that."

I remember sitting in stunned silence. My mother continued.

"You know all the times I sang in churches and in vaudeville, my father never came to hear me sing and I was so disappointed when he wouldn't let me go to Hollywood."

She then told me a version of the story I had never heard.

" 'Why won't you let me go to Hollywood,' I asked him."

" 'Hollywood's no place for a young woman,' he said."

"Why not?"

"Because you might have to go to bed with the guy who's running the show."

"So what?" I said. "He got mad and walked out of the room. My father never stayed in an argument, he just walked away. Oh, how I wish I had gone the way I wanted to. I screwed up my life."

I was fully aware that her normal "but I wouldn't have had you" justification was absent from the story. I took the omission to mean that she was no longer hiding from the pain her father had caused her. I felt relieved; I no longer had the burden of being responsible for fulfilling her life.

"That sounds painful, Mom," I said. She didn't reply; she just stared straight ahead giving me the impression that it was too painful for her in her eighty-fourth year to admit that she spent her life fulfilling others' expectations of her, but none of her own.

I began to see my mother in a different light. She was starved for love and affection and as a result never developed her own personality. She couldn't give me the love I needed because she didn't have it to give; she never got it in the first place. All her stories about her and her father probably represented what she hoped he would be and not what he was. It is interesting that I forgot about this conversation until I discovered the notes. Why would I forget something like that? It was a powerful conversation, and I remember telling my wife about it when I came home from visiting my mother. Maybe it was because it was the only story she told me about her father that was negative. All through my life, I had heard nothing but praise and love for this man. This story was so unusual, so unlike my mother that I had difficulty absorbing the new information. On the other hand, maybe I didn't want to remember it. My image of him sexually abusing her might have been more my need to see her suffer in retaliation for what she did to me. As long as she suffered as I did, as long as she got what was coming to her even if it was only in my mind, I could begin to let her go, or more profoundly, empathize with her as I so desperately had hoped she would empathize with me.

My grandfather may not have sexually abused my mother, but he and my grandmother did abuse her by withholding their emotional support and love. The lack of affection from her parents devastated this cute, adorable little girl. She probably wondered what was wrong with her, which created in her thousands of doubts about herself and prevented her from being the person God wanted her to be, just as I had been prevented. It may explain why she couldn't get too close to a man. She flirted but as soon as intimacy became an issue, she pulled away. Her father and mother never demonstrated what true intimacy was like. Of course, her parents didn't receive love and emotional support from their families, either. Regardless of which scenario is true, it changes nothing; my mother and I were still hurt children walking on the face of the earth looking for love, redemption, and the fulfillment of our dreams.

Forgiving my mother, however, would not have been possible without the power of God. If we do not call on God, human forgiveness is impossible. Some things can't be done by trying harder. I was brutally honest with God. I told God I thought he had devised a lousy system, and that I didn't want to forgive my mother. I laid down the gauntlet. I said, "God, if you want me to forgive, you will have to give me the power because I can't do it by myself." And God did. To forgive is to intentionally surrender yourself to God, to give up all claims to your life, and let God melt you, mold you, fill you, and use you. It's not easy, but in the end you can live life free in the grace, love, and mercy of God.

Epilogue

While I had forgiven my mother and lived to tell about it, and while this act did more for me than her, this didn't mean that feelings of warmth and love for her returned. I had empathy for her, I realized we were more alike than different, and I did love her as my mother who gave me life. The years of abuse left their toll, however, and while I could forgive her, I couldn't forget what she had done. There is the mistaken notion that forgiveness entails forgetting. You can't forget and you shouldn't forget. Jewish people refuse to forget the holocaust, just as African-Americans refuse to forget slavery, and rightfully so. To forget means that you declare the person or persons who did you harm, innocent, which is not true. It also has the potential to do you psychological harm because the act of forgetting a wrong requires repression of the pain, which in turn can be acted out in further self-destructive behavior and harm to others. While I can't forget what my mother did, nevertheless, in my forgiveness of her I determined that I would never let any harm come to her, and if necessary I would bring her to my home to care for her. Fortunately, she qualified for Medicaid in the State of New Mexico, and that along with her Social Security paid for her being at the Mission Arch Care Center that provided her with excellent care in the last years of her life.

I also prayed for my mother. Jesus says we are to pray for our enemies. Praying for another makes them more human and helps us to see ourselves in them. Surprisingly, I found myself praying one day that she die. I said to God, "She no longer has quality of life and we will never have the relationship we could have had, so for her sake take her home with you so she can see the full forgiveness and love you have in store for all of us. When I come to join you, you can reconcile us."

At first, I felt ashamed of praying for my mother's death. Was this my final revenge? On the other hand, I had moved beyond revenge and now was concerned about her welfare and knew that God was able to do that which we are not able to do. I was not asking God to harm her, but to forgive and restore her. I was not asking God to eliminate her as my mother but to transform her and give her the love she always needed so that one day we would be able to be mother and son as God intended. On January 6, 2005, about a year after I started praying for her death, the nursing home called. Wanda, her nurse, told me that she developed a blood clot in her lower right leg and the doctor said that her death was less than twenty-four hours away. He gave her medication to keep her out of pain. The next day she died. I thanked God for taking her, asked God to forgive us both, and sang, *Amazing Grace*.

I said in the preface that I learned that Jesus was right when Peter asked how many times we must forgive. Peter suggests seven times. This was quite a generous offer on Peter's part because the number "seven" in the Bible is a holy number, much like the number forty as in forty days and nights. The number is not to indicate an exact time but a perfect time, God's time. The number seven indicates an infinite number of times. Jesus refutes Peter, however, by saying, "Not seven times, but seventy times seven."[1] Even though Peter's offer is for an infinite number of times, Jesus refuses to put any limits on the need to forgive.

I say this because while I have forgiven my parents, a situation or a memory will make me recall the pain of my relationship with them, and I have to forgive all over again. I will hear about abused children, and I will be angry again with my parents. On the other hand, I might hear of people who had wonderful childhoods with loving and supportive parents, and I become jealous, and the anger I have for my parents resurfaces. Again, I'm called to forgive. Forgiveness is not a one-time act; it's an eternal act. The good news is that once you do forgive, successive acts of forgiveness become easier. I'm constantly forgiving my parents, as I trust I'm constantly being forgiven.

---

1. Matt 18:22.

Appendix

Note: The following is a sermon I preached on forgiveness. It recounts in a short space what I have said in this book. I offer it to fellow clergy in hopes that they will find it helpful in their own preaching. You may use any of the material in the sermon so long as you give proper credit to the author.

Forgiveness: The Struggle of the Soul
A Sermon by
Dr. Walter R. Smith
Preached at First Presbyterian Church
Lynchburg, Virginia
November 13, 2005
Scripture: Genesis 15:14–21;
Matthew 18:21–22; Luke 17:3–4

THE HEALTH SURVEY OF our congregation that was taken this past May by the Health Ministry Team of the Care and Nurture Committee in partnership with Centra Health's Pastoral Care Department has yielded valuable information about the physical and spiritual health of our congregation. The Health Ministry Team is using that information to help plan programs of interest in the area of physical and spiritual health, and today's sermon on forgiveness is in response to the spiritual question concerning forgiveness. A copy of those responses is in your bulletin this morning.

While the overall responses to the spiritual questions show a strong sense of spiritual well-being, the question that received the lowest positive response was, "I find it easy to forgive others." When you consider that one of the cornerstones of the Christian faith is forgiveness, the response to this question shows that forgiveness is something that does not come easily. If it did, the responses should have been right up there with the question "God has meaning in my life."

Forgiveness is hard, especially when we have been terribly hurt by a parent, relative, friend, business partner, or some physical attack on our personhood by a criminal. The pain of such an act is not something that is easily overcome. In many cases it takes years, and in some cases it is downright impossible. Forgiveness is the struggle of the soul. To forgive requires courage, the suffering of pain, the willingness to stand naked before God, and to ask God for help. There is nothing harder to do than to forgive a great wrong. It will test every ounce of your faith, but it will also give you a peace that no one can take from you. Hopefully, in this sermon we can come to some understanding of what forgiveness is, why we need to forgive, how we can forgive, and the benefits of forgiveness. I will share with you my own struggle to forgive others, especially my parents.

What is forgiveness? Biblically speaking, forgiveness is the loving, voluntary, cancellation of a debt. Jesus in the parable of the merciful servant tells about a king who wants to call in the debts of his slaves. One of his slaves owes him ten thousand talents. A talent was worth more than fifteen years' wages of a laborer. The slave could not pay and the king was about to have him, his family, and possessions sold when the slave begged him for more time promising to pay him all that he owed. The king in his mercy forgave or canceled completely the debt of the slave.

My own definition of forgiveness is a little different, but its effect is the same. I believe that we forgive when we let go of the pain of the hurt that has been done to us, so that we can reclaim our lives, restore our relationship to those who harmed us, and live in the joy and grace of God knowing that we have not only forgiven, but more importantly that we are forgiven by God.

Well, why should we forgive? Obviously, because Jesus tells us to forgive. Matthew, chapter 18, is devoted to how we as Christians live together in this community of faith. Peter wants to know how many times we must forgive each other, and he suggests seven times. This is a very generous offer on Peter's part because the number "seven" is a symbolic number that is often used to indicate infinity. However, what Peter was trying to do was to quantify forgiveness. He wanted a specific number of times to forgive after which you didn't have to pay attention to forgiving. But Jesus decimates that kind of thinking by saying, no, not an infinite number of times but an infinite, infinite number of times. You must always forgive. Forgiveness is something that must become a part of you; it must be as natural as breathing. So you can't put any quantity on the number of times you must forgive.

Forgiveness is one of the hallmarks of Jesus' ministry. Jesus forgave those who crucified him. He tells us that if we forgive anyone, God will forgive that person, too, and if we don't God will not forgive them either. He also says that if we forgive others, God will forgive us. These are difficult passages to understand. It almost seems as if God is turning his control of forgiveness over to us and will only do what we do, and that our forgiveness from God depends upon us forgiving others. But we can't control God; we can't tell or direct God what to do, and God is not beholden to our actions. If God waited for us to forgive others, God would never have sent Jesus Christ into the world. I think a better way to understand these passages is to see that their intent is to link our forgiveness with that of God's. Because God forgives, it becomes our responsibility to forgive, also. We cannot escape from our responsibility to live out our lives as the people of God. It is what the writer of I John means when he says, "Those who say, 'I love God,' and hate their brothers or sisters, are liars; for those who do not love a brother or sister whom they have seen, cannot love God whom they have not seen."[1] If we cannot strive to be God-like, even though we know we will fail, then we cannot be the people of God. We must try to imitate the nature of God. Another way to look at this is to realize that a great benefit of going through the struggle of forgiving others is that we will come to understand more fully the depth of God's forgiveness. The more we forgive others, the more we know that God forgives us. God's forgiveness and our forgiveness go hand-in-hand.

A non-Biblical reason to forgive is that we forgive not so much for the other person's sake but for our own. We often think that forgiving does more for the one who has hurt us than it does for us, and that may be the biggest impediment to our ability to forgive. Why should I do something for someone who has been so hurtful to me? It's like I'm giving up all my power to this person. I feel ashamed enough as it is by what he or she has done that the idea of doing something more for him or her becomes sickening. But true forgiveness does more for us than it does for those whom we forgive. Let me explain.

Dr. Glenn Mack Harnden, a Kansas psychologist, says that forgiveness releases us from prolonged anger, rage, and stress that have been linked to physiological problems such as cardiovascular disease, hypertension, arthritic conditions, cancer, and psychosomatic illnesses. People,

---

1. 1 John 4:20.

he said, who have these diseases may need to forgive someone or be forgiven. This is not true in every case, but it does indicate that not forgiving can produce negative effects on our health. The benefits of forgiveness are not only that we come to a deeper understanding of God's forgiveness, but that we will help create the conditions that allow us to live healthier lives in the joy and grace of God. That is important because the person we are forgiving may not care if they are forgiven or they may not feel they need forgiveness. If that is the case, and we go to all the trouble to forgive them, and our gift is not received well, then where does that leave us? I remember a time I told my mother that I forgave her for something hurtful she did to me. Her response was, "What do you mean forgive? I haven't done anything wrong; you're the one who has the problem." This does not mean we should never share our forgiveness with the person who has hurt us, but just to be aware that it may not be welcomed. So forgiveness cannot be just for the other person; it has to do something for us; it has to make us better people so that we become more the people God wants us to be.

How do we forgive? First, it may help to realize that forgiveness is a process; it's not an act. In other words, it is something that evolves and does not happen all at once. We might find that we are able to forgive a little bit today, some more in a year from now, still some more in years to come, and finally one day we will have forgiven completely. Then we will find that we still have to forgive because things will happen to us that will remind us of the hurt we experienced and we have to forgive all over again. This is one way to interpret Jesus' saying that we must forgive seventy seven times or seventy times seven. In other words, forgiveness is an eternal process. So don't feel badly if you can't forgive all at once. Don't feel badly if you haven't been able to forgive for years. It took me almost sixty years to forgive my parents, and I am still forgiving them. Don't get discouraged. Rather, confess your inability to forgive to God, and ask God to forgive the offending party for you. When I was in the process of forgiving my mother, I said to God, "God, I cannot forgive her, I don't want to forgive her, but I also know that what is not possible with me is possible with you. So will you forgive her for me today and work on me so that I can come to the place where I will be able to forgive her?" Don't hesitate to call on God to do some of the heavy lifting—Jesus says, "Come to me, all who labor and are heavy laden, and I will give you rest."[2]

2. Matt 11:28.

When we think of forgiveness, we usually think of forgiving someone else. We seldom think that we might be the ones that need the most forgiveness. In my journey of forgiving my parents, the person I had to forgive first was me. That's because children who grow up in dysfunctional homes see themselves as being the cause of the dysfunction. For example, I reasoned that my father neglected me because he was disappointed in me as a son. If I were a better son, he would have paid attention to me. So I grew up thinking that I was not good and it was me who caused my father to neglect me. I felt ashamed for not being a better son. At a young age, I didn't have the ability to see that it was his parents who beat him that caused him to act the way he did. I had to learn I was not the cause of his neglecting me, and in an ironic twist, I had to forgive myself for doing something that I did not do, but thought I did. Because we blamed ourselves in childhood, we are more likely to blame ourselves in adulthood when someone hurts us. We automatically think that they hurt us because of something we did, when in most cases it has nothing to do with what we did. People hurt other people more because of their own inner conflicts and hurts than because of what the other person has done. It was not until I forgave myself that I was able to begin the journey of forgiving my father and mother.

The hardest part of forgiving, however, is trying to understand the life of the person who hurt you and what conflicts they have or had in their lives. This is difficult because it requires that you give up all your preconceived ideas of this person you detest, and open yourself to the possibility that what caused them to hurt you was their own hurt and it had nothing to do with you. You open yourself to the possibility that after years of thinking they did not love you, they did, but they didn't know how to show it. You open yourself to the possibility that they might not have been as bad as you thought, and that you are more like them than different from them. And part of the process of forgiving is admitting that we can be as hurtful to others as others have been hurtful to us. This is especially difficult because the last thing we want to do is to find out that we are like the person we don't like.

One day five or six years ago, a fellow counselor who knew my struggle in forgiving my mother challenged me to think about what my mother's life was like as child. I didn't want to do it—why should I do it after all the hurt she caused me. My friend kept the pressure on me. I knew I had to do it, but I told God I didn't want to do it, and if I did it, I would need all the help God could give. Since I like to write, I wrote a story of what my mother's childhood might have been like. At the end of the story, I started to weep because I had just written a story of seven year-old girl who had been abused by her father and other members of the family and was never allowed to achieve her potential. The hurt little boy in me could identify with the hurt little girl in my mother, and I realized that like my father, my mother's life was probably more painful than my own. While that did not excuse my parents for what they did, I came to realize that they did the best they could for me with what they had been given. I was more like my parents than different from them because we were hurt little children walking on this earth together. I also had to admit that I had done my share of hurting my family and others. It was at that point, that I felt the pain, anger, and stress over not being able to forgive melt away. I began to live more fully in the joy and the grace of God as I realized that I had forgiven my parents.

However, none of this would have been possible without the power of God. If we do not call on God, human forgiveness is impossible. Some things cannot be done by trying harder. I was brutally honest with God. I told God I thought he had devised a lousy system, and that I didn't want to forgive. And I laid down the gauntlet. I said, "God if you want me to forgive, you will have to give me the power because I can't do it by myself." And God did. To forgive is to intentionally surrender yourself to God, and let God melt you, mold you, fill you, and use you. It's not easy, but in the end you can live life free in the grace, love, and mercy of God.

To God be the glory. Amen.

www.ingramcontent.com/pod-product-compliance
Lightning Source LLC
Chambersburg PA
CBHW060820190426
43197CB00038B/2167